The Official Story of The Championships

WIMBLEDON
2014

MONDAY 23RD JUNE
TO SUNDAY 6TH JULY 2014

WIMBLEDON.COM

Wimbledon
2014

The Official Story of The Championships
WIMBLEDON 2014

By Paul Newman

(Left) *The official 2014 Championships poster was designed by ESPN competition winner David Bartholow from Los Angeles, USA*

Published in 2014 by Vision Sports Publishing Ltd

Vision Sports Publishing Ltd
19-23 High Street, Kingston upon Thames
Surrey, KT1 1LL
www.visionsp.co.uk

ISBN: 978-1909534-24-7

Written by: Paul Newman
Additional writing by: Alexandra Willis
Edited by: Jim Drewett and Alexandra Willis
Production editor: Paul Baillie-Lane
Designed by: Neal Cobourne
Photography: Bob Martin, Thomas Lovelock, Jon Buckle, Dillon Bryden, Florian Eisele, Javier Garcia, Scott Heavey, David Levenson, Chris Raphael and Billie Weiss
Picture research: Paul Weaver, Neil Turner and Sarah Frandsen

All photographs © AELTC

Results and tables are reproduced courtesy of the AELTC

The All England Lawn Tennis Club (Championships) Limited
Church Road, Wimbledon, London, SW19 5AE, England
Tel: +44 (0)20 8944 1066
Fax: +44 (0)20 8947 8752
www.wimbledon.com

Printed in Slovakia by Neografia

This book is reproduced with the assistance of Rolex.

CONTENTS

FOREWORD
By Philip Brook
Chairman of The All England Lawn Tennis & Croquet Club and
Committee of Management of The Championships

At 2pm on Sunday 6 July, Roger Federer and Novak Djokovic walked through the doors to the entrance to Centre Court. Above the doors is an excerpt from Rudyard Kipling's poem, "If you can meet with triumph and disaster and treat those two impostors just the same". Little did they know that, over the next four hours, they would each have their own share of triumph and disaster in a gladiatorial tussle of the highest standards before Djokovic finally triumphed 6-4 in the deciding set. At 4-4 in the final set, Federer was just two games away from holding the outright record of eight Gentlemen's Singles wins. But then Djokovic came back.

Our congratulations to Novak on winning his second Gentlemen's Singles title, and also to Petra Kvitova on winning her second Ladies' Singles title. Petra overpowered Canada's rising star Eugenie Bouchard 6-3, 6-0 in just 55 minutes in what was arguably one of the finest displays of aggressive yet controlled tennis ever seen on Centre Court.

The 128th Championships reminded us once again that our sport never stands still. Who would have thought that some of the most talked about players this year would be Bouchard, Halep, Dimitrov, Kyrgios, Raonic, Sock and Pospisil. All of them are to be congratulated on their outstanding performances at this year's Championships – we will be hearing a lot more of these exciting talents in the years ahead.

In the weeks leading up to The Championships we concluded the sale of the 2016–2020 issue of Centre Court Debentures with over 90 per cent of our existing Debenture holders renewing their holdings. The issue raised just over £100 million, all of which will be used in our Master Plan to further improve the grounds at Wimbledon, including a new retractable roof on No.1 Court by 2019. We are very grateful to our Centre Court Debenture holders for their continued support and loyalty, which will help us to ensure that Wimbledon remains the finest stage in world tennis.

We look forward to the 2015 Championships and the addition of a third week of grass court tennis in the lead up to Wimbledon. The extra week will allow players more time for the important transition from clay to grass and additional opportunities for them to compete on grass ahead of The Championships. I hope this annual will bring back many happy memories of Wimbledon 2014.

INTRODUCTION
By Paul Newman

If the scenario had not been a familiar one, those of us who visited the All England Club barely four months before the start of The Championships 2014 might have been concerned. What had been the site of Courts 14 and 15 was now a huge hole in the ground, with concrete and ironwork structures sprouting out of it. There was a similar scene of disruption – and a gaping hole in the road – behind the Millennium Building.

However, as always the Club's timing in its building programme was as sweet as a Roger Federer forehand. By the first day of The Championships, the only visible trace of major change since last year was a notice informing the public that Courts 14 and 15, which by that time had been newly grassed, would not be in use in 2014. Beneath the courts will be new facilities for The Championships' personnel and the media, which will be fully operational next year, while the work in Somerset Road will provide new underground access to the Club.

For all the impression of timelessness that might come across at The Championships, the All England Club is always looking to innovate and improve. For example, in five years' time (planning applications and building programmes permitting), there will be a retractable roof on No.1 Court as part of the Wimbledon Master Plan. Before then, however, another major change will be in place. The Championships 2014 were the last to start only a fortnight after the French Open. Next year, there will be a three-week gap between Roland Garros and Wimbledon, giving players a greater chance to recover from the gruelling clay court season and more time to hone their grass court game.

There will be no repeat of Rafael Nadal's experiences this year, when he played (and lost) his first match on grass, at Halle, only four days after winning the French Open, and arrived at the All England Club having had precious little time to adjust to the surface. The short hiatus between Roland Garros and Wimbledon had long been a source of frustration, and the All England Club's bold decision to address it by moving The Championships back a week has been widely welcomed.

If Nadal went into The Championships 2014 "under-cooked", then Federer appeared to be coming to the boil. The seven-times Gentlemen's Singles Champion won the grass court tournament in Halle just eight days before the start of Wimbledon. Novak Djokovic had been pushing Nadal hard at the top of the world rankings, though he had again chosen not to compete before Wimbledon.

Andy Murray had won the Aegon Championships one year earlier en route to his Wimbledon triumph, but this time made an early exit from The Queen's Club. Grigor Dimitrov, took the title instead. Might this be the year when Dimitrov, his fellow 23-year-old, Milos Raonic, or the French Open semi-finalist, Ernests Gulbis, made their breakthrough?

New faces had also been making their mark in the women's game. Eugenie Bouchard, who had won the girls' title at The Championships two years earlier, had made the semi-finals at the Australian Open and French Open, where 22-year-old Simona Halep reached her first Grand Slam final. Garbine Muguruza had shocked Serena Williams in Paris, while Madison Keys had just claimed the biggest win of her career in Eastbourne.

With Williams and Li Na, No.1 and No.2 in the world respectively, beginning to waver, might this be time for a younger woman to create shockwaves in the way that 17-year-old Maria Sharapova had announced her talent by winning Wimbledon 10 years previously? Come to think of it, might this be the moment for Sharapova to win her second All England Club title? It was time to find out.

WIMBLEDON 2014

Gentlemen's Singles Seeds

Novak Djokovic (Serbia)
Seeded 1st
Age: 27
Wimbledon titles: 1
Grand Slam titles: 7

Rafael Nadal (Spain)
Seeded 2nd
Age: 28
Wimbledon titles: 2
Grand Slam titles: 14

Andy Murray (Great Britain)
Seeded 3rd
Age: 27
Wimbledon titles: 1
Grand Slam titles: 2

Roger Federer (Switzerland)
Seeded 4th
Age: 32
Wimbledon titles: 7
Grand Slam titles: 17

Stan Wawrinka (Switzerland)
Seeded 5th
Age: 29
Grand Slam titles: 1

Tomas Berdych (Czech Republic)
Seeded 6th
Age: 28

David Ferrer (Spain)
Seeded 7th
Age: 32

Milos Raonic (Canada)
Seeded 8th
Age: 23

9th John Isner (USA)
10th Kei Nishikori (Japan)
11th Grigor Dimitrov (Bulgaria)
12th Ernests Gulbis (Latvia)

13th Richard Gasquet (France)
14th Jo-Wilfried Tsonga (France)
15th Jerzy Janowicz (Poland)
16th Fabio Fognini (Italy)

THE SEEDS
Ladies' Singles Seeds

Serena Williams
(USA)
Seeded 1st
Age: 32
Wimbledon titles: 5
Grand Slam titles: 17

Li Na
(China)
Seeded 2nd
Age: 32
Grand Slam titles: 2

Simona Halep
(Romania)
Seeded 3rd
Age: 22

Agnieszka
Radwanska
(Poland)
Seeded 4th
Age: 25

Maria
Sharapova
(Russia)
Seeded 5th
Age: 27
Wimbledon titles: 1
Grand Slam titles: 5

Petra Kvitova
(Czech
Republic)
Seeded 6th
Age: 24
Wimbledon titles: 1
Grand Slam titles: 1

Jelena Jankovic
(Serbia)
Seeded 7th
Age: 29

Victoria
Azarenka
(Belarus)
Seeded 8th
Age: 24
Grand Slam titles: 2

9th Angelique Kerber (Germany)
10th Dominika Cibulkova (Slovakia)
11th Ana Ivanovic (Serbia)
12th Flavia Pennetta (Italy)

13th Eugenie Bouchard (Canada)
14th Sara Errani (Italy)
15th Carla Suarez Navarro (Spain)
16th Caroline Wozniacki (Denmark)

DAY ONE
MONDAY 23 JUNE

T here is always something special about the first day at The Championships. Of course, players, coaches and officials all feel it, but so do the crowd. A sense of anticipation fills the air and there is an extra spring in spectators' steps as they walk up Church Road. The great adventure of the next Wimbledon fortnight is about to begin – and they will be there to share in it.

David Goffin (left) and Andy Murray (right) walk out to open Centre Court on day one of Wimbledon 2014

For those who regularly undertake this pilgrimage, there is the warm feeling of familiarity and of timelessness: every year there are physical developments and innovations at the All England Club, but the soul of SW19 never changes. Even for a seasoned visitor the excitement of the first day remains undiminished, fed by the joy of renewing their acquaintance with the surroundings, of recalling past delights and of anticipating what is to come. For those making their debut visit, there is a sense of wonder, enhanced by the first glimpses of Centre Court and No.1 Court on the approach to the All England Club. It can feel as though the tide of people on the streets is heading in only one direction.

The scene may be unchanging, but on this occasion there was something very different to look forward to. Andy Murray had ended Britain's 77-year wait for a Gentlemen's Singles Champion the previous summer. Now the country had the chance to welcome back a homegrown defending Gentlemen's Singles Champion for the first time in 78 years; Fred Perry, who won the last of his three Wimbledon titles in 1936, did not return the following year because he had turned professional.

It is one of Wimbledon's best loved traditions – and one which is not repeated at the other three Grand Slam tournaments – that the previous year's Gentlemen's Singles Champion begins the defence of his title in the opening match on Centre Court on the first day. It brings an element of ceremony to the occasion and reinforces the sense of history. Murray had been asked countless times in the build-up to Wimbledon what he thought the experience might be like as he walked out on Centre Court as defending champion for the first time. He invariably answered that he had little idea because it had never happened to him before. He knew, however, how he felt about his chances of retaining his title. "I'm here to try and win the tournament," Murray had told the media that day. "I trained hard the last 10 days or so. Preparation's gone well, so it's now down to me to try and perform on the court."

The 50 weeks since that magical day on Centre Court had not always been easy for Murray. After undergoing back surgery in September, he did not play again in 2013. His subsequent comeback, which peaked with a run to the French Open semi-finals, had been steady if unspectacular (he had not won a tournament since last year's Championships) and had been disrupted by a parting of the ways with his coach, Ivan Lendl. Just 15 days before his opening match at Wimbledon he had announced the appointment of Amelie Mauresmo as his coach on a trial basis for the grass court season. As the first reigning male Grand Slam singles champion in history to appoint a female coach other than a family member, the Scot created headlines around the world, fuelling further interest in his attempt to defend his Wimbledon crown.

Mauresmo was one of the few people who could give Murray an idea of what it would be like to defend a Wimbledon title, but surely not even the Ladies' Singles Champion of 2006 could have predicted the reception given to her new charge when he walked out to face Belgium's David Goffin on a warm and sunlit afternoon. Cheers and applause rang around Centre Court as Murray was given a prolonged standing ovation. In past years it had taken time for the Wimbledon crowd to take Murray to their hearts, but now they energetically showed their appreciation for the defending champion. Among those watching from the Royal Box were Murray's grandparents and his father, not to mention American basketball icon, Shaquille O'Neal, and F1 legend, Sir Jackie Stewart.

From the moment Murray raced into a 3-0 lead, he never looked in danger of joining Manuel Santana (in 1967) or Lleyton Hewitt (in 2003) as the only defending men's champions to go out in the first round. Goffin, a fresh-faced 23 year old, looked as nervous as a young West End understudy on opening night and was given a sympathetic round of applause when he finally got on the scoreboard.

Andy Murray in practice as new coach Amelie Mauresmo looks on

The world No.105 improved in the latter stages, but Murray's 6-1, 6-4, 7-5 victory was emphatic. For the most part it was a workmanlike display, but there was a sprinkling of brilliance, including a game-winning lob in the first set which brought a smile to Mauresmo's face. However, despite the resounding triumph Murray remained level headed about his performance. "I hit the ball very well," he said. "There weren't any moments where I felt like I was mistiming balls."

Novak Djokovic, the man Murray beat in last year's final, had not played a competitive match on grass since, but the No.1 seed opened his campaign in even more impressive fashion by beating Andrey Golubev 6-0, 6-1, 6-4. Like Murray, Djokovic had brought an entourage which included a familiar face on Centre Court, the Serb having appointed Boris Becker, three times a Wimbledon singles champion in the 1980s, as his head coach.

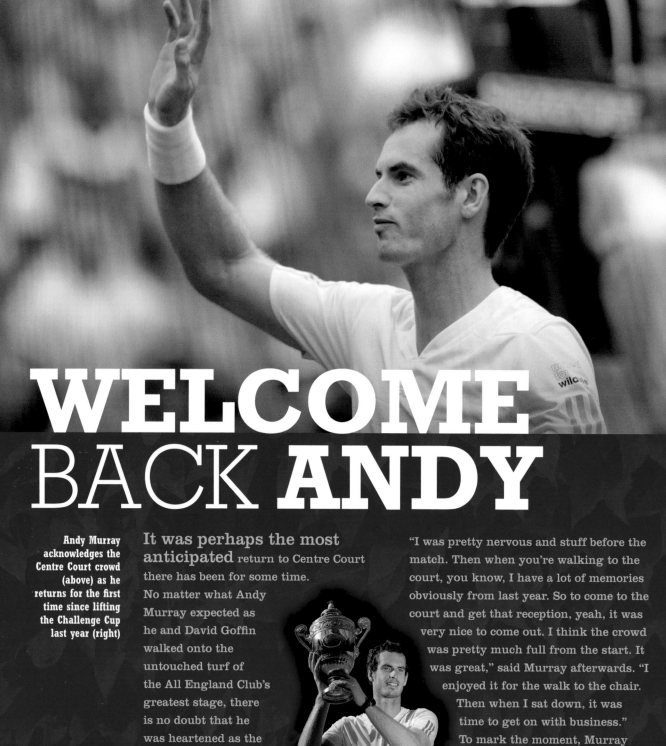

WELCOME BACK ANDY

Andy Murray acknowledges the Centre Court crowd (above) as he returns for the first time since lifting the Challenge Cup last year (right)

It was perhaps the most anticipated return to Centre Court there has been for some time. No matter what Andy Murray expected as he and David Goffin walked onto the untouched turf of the All England Club's greatest stage, there is no doubt that he was heartened as the Centre Court crowd rose to greet them, applauding as Murray waved in acknowledgement. As he sat down in his chair Murray briefly closed his eyes, taking in the atmosphere of the court that has brought him so much success.

"I was pretty nervous and stuff before the match. Then when you're walking to the court, you know, I have a lot of memories obviously from last year. So to come to the court and get that reception, yeah, it was very nice to come out. I think the crowd was pretty much full from the start. It was great," said Murray afterwards. "I enjoyed it for the walk to the chair. Then when I sat down, it was time to get on with business." To mark the moment, Murray and Wimbledon joined forces in a social media campaign. Anyone who tweeted #WelcomeBackAndy received a signed, personalised digital photo from the defending champion as a thank you for their support. Over 5,000 people took up the opportunity during a 24-hour window.

WIMBLEDON IN NUMBERS

1 Grand Slam match wins for former boys' singles champion Luke Saville, who won his first ever Grand Slam match with a respectable four-set victory over Dominic Thiem.

Sergiy Stakhovsky and Fernando Verdasco, who had both played significant roles a year earlier, had contrasting fortunes. Stakhovsky, who had condemned Roger Federer to his earliest exit for 11 years with his second-round victory, beat Argentina's Carlos Berlocq 6-3, 6-3, 6-3, while Verdasco, who went closer to beating Murray than anyone last year, in the quarter-finals, lost 4-6, 6-4, 4-6, 2-6 to Australia's Marinko Matosevic.

Fabio Fognini, the No.16 seed, produced the comeback of the day to beat Alex Kuznetsov 2-6, 1-6, 6-4, 6-1, 9-7. There was also rich entertainment on Court 12, where Marcos Baghdatis, a favourite of the Wimbledon faithful over the years, kissed the grass after knocking out Dustin Brown, who only a fortnight earlier had claimed the scalp of Rafael Nadal on grass at Halle. Jurgen Melzer and Bradley Klahn survived the first day, but only thanks to the weather. Melzer was trailing 1-6, 6-3, 6-3, 2-6, 4-5 to Jo-Wilfried Tsonga and Sam Querrey was about to serve for the match against Klahn when early evening rain brought both matches to a close for the day.

The first upset of The Championships had come on Court 18, where Sloane Stephens, the No.18 seed, was beaten 2-6, 6-7(8) by the unseeded Maria Kirilenko, who as the No.10 seed had fallen at the first hurdle to Britain's Laura Robson 12 months previously. Samantha Stosur, the No.17 seed, extended her run of Wimbledon disappointments when she was beaten 4-6, 3-6 by Belgium's Yanina Wickmayer. Venus Williams, five times a Ladies' Singles Champion here, won her first match at the All England Club for three years by beating Spain's Maria-Teresa Torro-Flor 6-4, 4-6, 6-2. Petra Kvitova, the 2011 champion and No.6 seed, found form immediately, defeating her fellow Czech, Andrea Hlavackova, 6-3, 6-0.

Naomi Broady beams as she completes her first victory in the main draw at Wimbledon

Naomi Broady joined Murray as a British winner on the first day, a 2-6, 7-6(7), 6-0 victory over Hungary's Timea Babos securing her place in the second round for the first time. Johanna Konta, the British No.3, pushed China's Peng Shuai hard before losing 4-6, 6-3, 4-6. All four of the British wild cards in action in the men's singles were knocked out. Nevertheless, Daniel Cox put up a spirited display to take a set off the world No.42, Jeremy Chardy. Dan Evans also won a set, against Andrey Kuznetsov, but James Ward and Kyle Edmund were beaten in straight sets by Mikhail Youzhny and Andreas Haider-Maurer respectively.

Ernests Gulbis, a great entertainer in the modern game, provided one of the day's most amusing moments after beating Jurgen Zopp. Gulbis was asked by a journalist for his view on John McEnroe's tongue-in-cheek comments about playing matches without umpires. "Get rid of vampires?" Gulbis asked. Having continued the discussion, if a little bemused, the Latvian finally realised that he had misheard the original question. "My God. Umpires? I thought something else. I thought vampires in the way the people who are surrounding and sucking the energy out of players. That's what I meant."

The Championships

Overnight Queue starts here **NOT** before 08.00 on Sunday 22nd June 2014

THE FIRST DAY RUSH

For the second year running, there was a queue for The Queue ahead of The Championships. Anyone who took a turn down Wimbledon Park Road on Saturday evening would have encountered a significant number of hardy individuals installed along the pavement, desperate to secure their spot before the official Queue opened in Wimbledon Park golf course at 8am on Sunday morning. It was worth their while by the time Monday morning arrived, as a total of 41,325 visitors to the Grounds enjoyed an action-packed day around the outside courts and on the Hill. The weather remained fair, with spots of sunshine at times, until a brief rain shower caused play to be suspended at 8pm. Still, it was a good day had by all.

Court
19

No Seats Reserved

COURT No.9

A. Kudryavtseva
B. Zahlavova Strycova

DAY TWO
TUESDAY 24 JUNE

In a mirror image of the opening day, it is tradition for the defending Ladies' Singles Champion to open proceedings on Centre Court on the first Tuesday. Marion Bartoli, the 2013 champion, was indeed present for Ladies' Day and walked on to the court in what was almost an all-white outfit, but, having retired last summer, less than two months after lifting the Venus Rosewater Dish, the Frenchwoman was wearing a cream lace dress and matching jacket rather than her tennis kit. Accompanied by nine-year-old Elle Robus-Miller from the Elena Baltacha Academy of Tennis, Bartoli took part in a special coin toss ceremony to celebrate the life of the former British No.1, who died in May 2014.

Sabine Lisicki follows through on a backhand in the first Ladies' match on Centre Court

The honour of playing the opening match instead fell to Sabine Lisicki, the runner-up in 2013. One year earlier the German had wept during the second set of the final, but this time it was Bartoli who shed the tears as she left the court to a warm ovation from the crowd and took her seat in the Royal Box. The intervening 12 months had not gone as Lisicki might have hoped, though. Struggling to recover from a shoulder injury, she arrived at the All England Club having only once won two matches in a row in 2014. Nevertheless, there appeared to be nothing like the smell of freshly mown grass to revive Lisicki's spirits. The previous day she had watched video clips of the 2013 final to remind herself of the biggest day of her career and "to calm down the nerves". On this occasion it was Lisicki's opponent, Julia Glushko, a 24-year-old Israeli making her Wimbledon debut, who had difficulty handling the pressure. Without ever needing to find her best tennis, Lisicki showed how comfortable she can be on grass, winning 6-2, 6-1. "This is such a special place to me, it always has been," the German said afterwards. "I love that court so much. It definitely helped me. The crowd as well helped me to settle very quickly."

Serena Williams knows what it is like to arrive as the defending champion, but her most recent memory of Centre Court had been a less enjoyable one. Twelve months earlier the five-times Ladies' Singles Champion had lost to Lisicki in the fourth round in one of the biggest upsets of the Fortnight that year. Having arrived at Wimbledon on the back of another shock defeat, to Garbine Muguruza in the second round of the French Open, questions were asked whether Williams might be short on confidence as she wound up the day's Centre Court programme against Georgian-turned-American, Anna Tatishvili. Within 61 minutes we had the answer, the world No.1 delivering 16 aces en route to a 6-1, 6-2 victory. Meanwhile Eugenie Bouchard, a semi-finalist at the Australian and French Opens, cleared a tricky first hurdle by beating the experienced Daniela Hantuchova 7-5, 7-5.

The Championships always provide some intriguing match-ups and there could hardly have been more contrasting opponents than the two ladies who contested the third match on No.1 Court. Maria Sharapova, the world's highest-earning sportswoman and one of the biggest names in tennis, was back at the All England Club 10 years after stunning the game with her victory over Serena Williams in the final at the age of just 17. This time her opponent was Samantha Murray, a 26-year-old Briton who was returning as a tennis pro after working in The Championships' accreditation office seven years previously. Last year Sharapova's annual earnings were estimated by *Forbes* magazine at $29 million, while Murray started their match having won prize money of less than $131,000 in her whole career. The world No.247 had the support of Andy Murray – her uncle shares the same name as the 2013 Gentlemen's Singles Champion – and was given every encouragement by a supportive crowd, but it was no surprise when Sharapova won 6-1, 6-0. "It was a great experience," Murray said afterwards. "I've only been on the court before as a fan."

Britain's Heather Watson provided home supporters with a victory, overcoming Ajla Tomljanovic, a 21 year old from Croatia who had recently beaten Agnieszka Radwanska at Roland Garros. Watson, who won 6-3, 6-2, had arrived in fine form, having reached the semi-finals of the Aegon International in Eastbourne the previous week. However, the world No.60 admitted that she had been so nervous before going out on No.3 Court that her jaw had locked as she tried to eat a banana. The 22 year old from Guernsey, who had climbed 101 places in the world rankings in the previous four months after making a spirited recovery from glandular fever, had woken up at 4am on the day of the match. "I was

Heather Watson acknowledges the crowd after an impressive first-round win

ready to go, but I actually managed to get back to sleep," Watson said. Another Briton, Tara Moore, stood at one set apiece against Vera Zvonareva, the 2010 runner-up, when play was called off for the evening, while Dan Smethurst, the home country's last wild card in the gentlemen's singles, was far from disgraced in going down 5-7, 3-6, 4-6 to the big-serving American, John Isner.

Australian tennis has not had much to celebrate in recent years, but day one had brought the promise of a better future with victories for Bernard Tomic, Marinko Matosevic, Luke Saville, Casey Dellacqua and Jarmila Gajdosova. Wins for Lleyton Hewitt and Nick Kyrgios on day two meant that seven Australians had reached the second round,

RALLYING FOR BALLY

The coin toss ahead of the first match of the Ladies' Singles Championship on Centre Court, performed by defending champion Marion Bartoli, was not just to determine whether Sabine Lisicki or Julia Glushko would serve first. More symbolically, the occasion had also been chosen to celebrate the life of former British No.1 Elena Baltacha, who died from liver cancer in May, less than a year after competing in The Championships in 2013. With husband Nino Severino and her family members watching in the stands, 'Bally', as she was fondly known, was represented by nine-year-old Elle Robus-Miller from the Elena

Baltacha Academy of Tennis (EBAT), who accompanied Bartoli on to Centre Court for the coin toss. Both proudly wearing the striking yellow (Baltacha's favourite colour) 'Rally for Bally' wristbands – sold at Wimbledon and throughout the grass court season to raise funds for the academy and for the Royal Marsden Cancer Charity – the Centre Court crowd rose to greet them and the special ceremony was a fitting tribute to a player who had always given her utmost at Wimbledon. Set up by the big-hearted Baltacha to give children of all backgrounds the opportunity to learn to play tennis, EBAT was described by Martina Navratilova, standing courtside for the coin toss, as "amazing." She continued: "To start the academy while she was still pro was amazing. Most players just want to rest in their spare time. It's important her dream lives on."
www.justgiving.com/RallyForBally

the most since 1999 when 10 had progressed beyond the first stage. Hewitt beat Poland's Michal Przysiezny 6-2, 6-7(14), 6-1, 6-4 in a typically battling display, to the delight of a lively group of Australian 'Fanatics' on No.3 Court. Kyrgios, at 19 the youngest man left in the draw, beat the veteran Frenchman Stéphane Robert 7-6(2), 7-6(1), 6-7(6), 6-2.

Rafael Nadal and Roger Federer both started The Championships hoping to erase painful memories from 2013, when the Spaniard lost in the first round to Steve Darcis and the Swiss fell in the second round to Sergiy Stakhovsky. Nadal, the champion in 2008 and 2010, had also made an early departure in 2012, losing to Lukas Rosol in the second round in what remains one of the biggest upsets in Grand Slam tennis. The world No.1 arrived at the All England Club as the US Open and French Open champion, but in his only competitive match on grass in the build-up he had lost to Dustin Brown in Halle. Martin Klizan, a 24-year-old Slovakian, was not the easiest of first-round opponents and, when the world No.51 won the first set, the Centre Court crowd's gasps were almost as loud as their cheers. Nadal eventually recovered to win 4-6, 6-3, 6-3, 6-3, but later admitted that the match had been "difficult". He added: "You need to find the routines again. You need to find the confidence on some shots. The only way for those things to come automatically is to play matches."

Federer, making his 16th successive appearance at The Championships and extending his Open era record to 59 consecutive Grand Slam tournaments, had no such difficulties. The seven-times Gentlemen's Singles Champion had prepared for Wimbledon in customary fashion by winning the title in Halle and still gave the impression that he could play on grass in his sleep. After beating a fellow 32-year-old, Italy's Paolo Lorenzi, 6-1, 6-1, 6-3 in his opening match, Federer said: "I feel 24. I can't believe how old I am already. The tennis life goes by in a flash."

Stan Wawrinka, the Australian Open champion, won only his second match in his last five visits to Wimbledon when he beat Portugal's Joao Sousa 6-3, 6-4, 6-3, while Jo-Wilfried Tsonga and Sam Querrey, who had been on the brink of victories when play was called off the previous evening, wasted little time in wrapping up their wins over Jurgen Melzer and Bradley Klahn respectively. Blink and you might have missed Tsonga's appearance on No.1 Court: the Frenchman needed to play only four more points before securing his place in the second round.

(Above) Gael Monfils throws his body into full flight in pursuit of a ball

(Below left) Stan Wawrinka pumps his fist after a much-needed first round win

WIMBLEDON IN NUMBERS

32 The number of aces produced by Ivo Karlovic during his first round match. But he still lost, falling 4-6, 6-7(5), 6-7(4) to Frank Dancevic.

SEEING DOUBLE

The outside courts at The Championships are unique for their openness. There are no walls or fences to hide the tennis behind, which makes for a remarkable scene when there are umpteen matches going on at once, as captured in this photograph.

PLAYERS ARE REMINDED THAT THE RULE:

"ALMOST ENTIRELY WHITE"
AND
"ACCEPTABLE TENNIS ATTIRE"

APPLIES TO:

ANY PERSON PLAYING AT ALL TIMES ON CHAMPIONSHIPS COURTS

PLEASE NOTE:

PLAYERS NOT CONFORMING TO THIS RULE WILL BE ASKED TO LEAVE THE COURT

ALL WHITE NOW

Wimbledon is famous for its dedication to tradition, and the practice of the players wearing white is one of the most well known. Keen-eyed observers at The Championships this year may have noticed even more unblemished white on display, the result of a tightening, or redefining, of the rules. The revised regulations cover all clothing and accessories, including tracksuits, sweaters, caps, undergarments and wristbands, worn on the Championship courts for practice and matches, though not on the Aorangi practice courts. Off-white and cream are not deemed to be white, and the only acceptable deviation on clothing is a single trim of colour no wider than 1cm. Shoes, including soles, must be almost entirely white. The only items which may be coloured, if absolutely necessary, are medical supports and equipment.

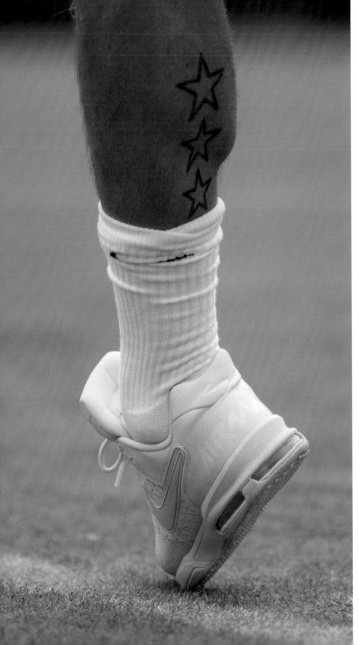

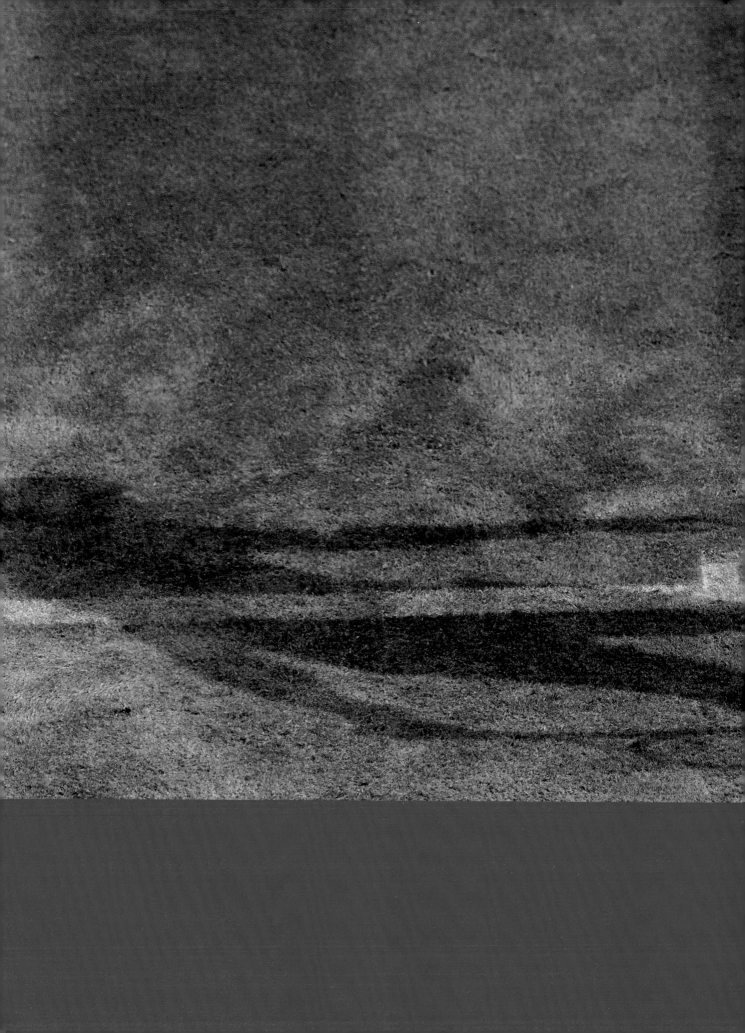

DAY THREE
WEDNESDAY 25 JUNE

Every now and then a match is played at Wimbledon that embodies the joy and the spirit of tennis. It might not be the most important encounter of The Championships and the outcome might not be exceptional, but such matches can lift the hearts of performers and spectators alike. For those lucky enough to have had seats on Centre Court for Novak Djokovic's second-round meeting with Radek Stepanek, this was such an occasion. Djokovic, as you would expect of the No.1 seed, emerged as the winner, but his 6-4, 6-3, 6-7(5), 7-6(5) victory will live long in the memory, not for the result but for the rich entertainment the two competitors provided.

Novak Djokovic grins at his team after a thrilling four-set win over Radek Stepanek

At the age of 35, Stepanek was the oldest player left in the gentlemen's singles, but he is still a fine player, especially on grass. Andy Murray could confirm this fact, having lost to the Czech at The Queen's Club a fortnight earlier. The former world No.8, who practises regularly with Djokovic, plays tennis from another era, caressing the ball around the court, working his way into a position of strength and moving in for the kill if the opportunity arises. He also knows how to play to the crowd. He cajoled officials, feigned exhaustion after long points and saved his best moment of theatre for last. On match point, when a Djokovic cross-court pass was called in, Stepanek challenged, went on his knees and held his hands in prayer, but to no avail.

The match was full of spectacular rallies. Djokovic was not quite at his best, but the Serb is a fine athlete and, with Stepanek throwing himself around the court, it made for great entertainment. Djokovic let slip an early lead in both tie-breaks and could have been taken to a decider had Stepanek not netted what should have been a routine volley at 5-5 in the second of them. There were moments when Stepanek's eye for drama might have got under Djokovic's skin, but for the most part the match was played in a wonderful spirit. At deuce in a key game in the fourth set, Djokovic sportingly conceded a point to Stepanek when he admitted that an incorrect call had not affected his subsequent missed shot. "It's fair play," Djokovic said later. "It's something that I would expect my opponent to do for me. Unfortunately, it doesn't happen very often."

At the end of the match the two men shared a long embrace at the net and then left the court together, signing autographs along the way. Before walking off, Stepanek bade a long farewell to the crowd, perhaps wondering whether he would ever grace this stage again. Djokovic agreed that there were some days which faded quickly from the memory, but this would not be one of them. "You remember certain matches that were special," he said. "Today's match went around three and a half hours, Centre Court, crowd involved, great points, a lot of entertainment. I'll definitely remember this match."

The equivalent day last year had been one of the most extraordinary in Wimbledon history. Roger Federer, Maria Sharapova and Victoria Azarenka were all beaten, and seven players withdrew or retired through injury. John McEnroe called it one of the "all-time craziest days". This time there were a handful of mild shocks, but they were minor tremors compared with last year's earthquakes. The highest ranked player to fall was the No.7 seed, David Ferrer, who in losing in the second round made his earliest exit from a Grand Slam tournament for more than four years. The 32-year-old Spaniard, a quarter-finalist in 2012 and 2013, was beaten 6-7(5), 6-0, 3-6, 6-3, 6-2 by Russia's Andrey Kuznetsov. Ernests Gulbis, the No.12 seed, was unable to build on his run to the semi-finals of the French Open and was beaten 4-6, 3-6, 6-7(5) by Sergiy Stakhovsky, who had knocked out Federer on the equivalent day last year. Azarenka suffered Wednesday woe for the second year in succession, though the No.8 seed's 3-6, 6-3, 5-7 loss to Serbia's Bojana Jovanovski was barely a surprise given that she was playing only her fourth match since January 2014 following a foot injury.

Li Na, Agnieszka Radwanska and Petra Kvitova, seeded second, fourth and sixth respectively, won their second-round matches for the loss of just 10 games between them. Kvitova's victory over Mona Barthel set up a heavyweight confrontation with Venus Williams, who reached the third round of a Grand Slam tournament for only the second time in three years by beating Japan's Kurumi Nara 7-6(4), 6-1. Later in the day, the five-times Ladies' Singles

Radek Stepanek gave his all against Novak Djokovic, throwing his body around the court and even over the net on one occasion

The Duchess of Cornwall meets Laura Robson and other players, while fellow Brit Tara Moore (top) came very close to victory against Vera Zvonareva

Champion teamed up with her sister, Serena, to beat Oksana Kalashnikova and Olga Savchuk 5-7, 6-1, 6-4 in the ladies' doubles. Britain's Tara Moore served for the match twice against Vera Zvonareva, but was broken on each occasion by the 2010 runner-up, who won 6-4, 6-7(3), 9-7, the match having resumed at the start of the third set after bad light had halted play the previous evening. Naomi Broady's 6-3, 6-2 defeat to Caroline Wozniacki left Heather Watson as the only Briton left in the ladies' singles.

Andy Murray was already the only home player still standing in the gentlemen's singles and never looked in danger against Blaz Rola, a 23 year old from Slovenia who had not played a tour-level match until 2014. Watched by the Duchess of Cornwall, who had left her seat in the Royal Box on Centre Court to see his match on No.1 Court, Murray recorded his most economical victory in his 46 matches at the All England Club's grass, winning 6-1, 6-1, 6-0 in just 84 minutes.

A champagne cork was heard to pop when Rola led in the opening game, but the world No.92 had few chances to celebrate thereafter. Rola had risen more than 400 places in the world rankings in the previous 12 months, but this was a huge step up in class for a man who was playing college tennis in the United States until last summer. Murray, who treated the crowd to a splendid display of shot-making, was delighted to win so quickly. At the French Open he felt he might have played better in his semi-final against Rafael Nadal if he had not had some long matches in the

Quiet Please
During Play

AELTC
Deep Water
No Bathing

**KEEP
OFF THE
GRASS**

Please do
not sit on
the plants

TAKE NOTE

The All England Club prides itself on giving spectators help and advice during their day at The Championships, with Honorary Stewards on hand to answer queries. There are also plenty of written instructions around and about the Grounds to help visitors avoid falling foul of any regulations. And most importantly, to keep off the grass.

Please Queue
Here

AELTC
In the interests of your own safety
please do not stand on this wall

Tents left
here will be
removed

**Quiet please
when play
in progress**

ANDY GETS HACKED!

Andy Murray is interviewed by the CBBC presenter, Hacker T. Dog, also known as Hacker the Dog. Hacker is operated by BAFTA-nominated puppeteer and comedian Phil Fletcher

As the Wimbledon Champion and British No.1, Andy Murray has been interviewed by many a famous face during his career, from Jonathan Ross to Holly Willoughby to James Corden and more. But on the third day of The Championships he joined the ranks of those to be grilled by CBBC celebrity, Hacker T. Dog, also known as Hacker the Dog, a Border Terrier from Wigan. Hacker makes a habit of tricking people into being interviewed by him on his show 'Hacker Time', one of his favourite victims being Sue Barker. Using all his wits, he managed to get Murray into an interview room, and was keen to ask him about his own pair of Border Terriers, Maggie May and Rusty, whether he had ever been to Wigan, and, most importantly, if Sue Barker, the object of his affections, ever mentioned him. "I did get a Christmas card from her you know," said Hacker to Murray. "Oh really, what did it say?" replied Andy, somewhat bemused. "There was a restraining order in it," the dog deadpanned. "I was furious." There followed... a joke. "What time does Roger Federer go to bed?" asked Hacker. "Tennish," quipped Murray. "Ten o'clock... tennis. Tennis. I meant TENNISH! Oh I got it wrong then..." continued Hacker. "Do you mind if I leave now? That's... that's enough," said Murray, escaping, much to Hacker's distress. "Andy, no! Andy, don't leave! Please whatever happens, don't. Murray... Andy. No! Andy Murray PLEASE... Well, on your way can you give John Inverdale a nudge if you see him in the corridor?" You can watch the interview in full on **Wimbledon.com** and **YouTube.com/Wimbledon**.

WIMBLEDON IN NUMBERS

82

Winners hit by Alexandr Dolgopolov during his 6-7(4), 7-6(0), 6-3, 6-4 win over Benjamin Becker. Forty-two of them were aces.

earlier rounds. "I didn't finish the sets off as best as I would have liked," he said of his fortnight in Paris. "I wanted to make sure here that when I had the momentum, when I was on top, that I finished the sets off. I did that well today."

All five Australians in singles competition lost, dampening the enthusiasm generated by their country's feats on the first two days, while Fabio Fognini experienced mixed fortunes. The Italian progressed to the third round at the expense of Germany's Tim Puetz, but learned that he had been fined a Wimbledon record $27,500 for his behaviour during his triumph over Alex Kuznetsov on the first day. Fognini was fined $20,000 for damaging the court with his racket, $7,500 for verbally abusing an official and $2,500 for making an obscene gesture. Meanwhile, it was a case of déjà vu for Jo-Wilfried Tsonga and Sam Querrey. Both men had first-round matches suspended late on Monday evening when they were on the brink of victory and returned to finish the job on day two. Day three saw the Frenchman and the American on opposite sides of the net and, surprise, surprise, play was called off shortly before 9.30pm with the two men tied at 9-9 in the fifth set.

(Above) Serena Williams is given assistance after running into the crowd during her doubles match, while Jo-Wilfried Tsonga and Sam Querrey were suspended due to failing light **(below)**

WIMBLEDON
AWAITS

#WIMBLEDON

Welcome
to Wimbledon

THE CHAMPIONSHIPS
WIMBLEDON

WIMBLEDON
AWAITS

DJOKOVIC AWAITS

Novak Djokovic has made the
semi-finals or better in his last
four Wimbledon appearances,
securing his first title in 2011.
Is 2014 the year for a
repeat performance?

TRADITION

HIPPOPOTENNIS
JOINS THE QUEUE

You might well ask: what does a hippo have to do with tennis? Each Championships, Wimbledon's Education Department runs a community art project, intended to visualise a particular behind-the-scenes aspect of the tournament for the visiting spectators. This year, having delved into the Wimbledon Compendium, the department set themselves the task of conveying the vast numbers of tennis balls, 54,250 to be precise, used on the match courts during the Fortnight. It just so happens that the weight of 54,250 tennis balls, 57.7g per ball, is equivalent to 3,100kg, which is... the weight of a hippo. Thus the Hippopotennis project was born, resulting in the creation of a full-sized adult hippo, made of papier mache, floating on a bed of water hyacinth, made from tennis balls. Created by local artist Maggie Ruddy, with the help of students at Wimbledon High School, the hippo, named

Horatio by Wimbledon's Twitter followers, took his place in the Queue. He became the ultimate photo opportunity, and a very different sort of attraction for those waiting patiently. Following the conclusion of The Championships, the hippo was moved inside the Grounds, taking up residence as an attraction on the daily tours of the Museum and the Grounds. You can follow the hippo's movements on Twitter at **@WimbledonHippo**.

Children pose with the hippo (below), which was situated next to Wimbledon's world-famous Queue (above). For the first time, the Queue featured five screens, in partnership with Stella Artois (middle left), to help visitors pass the time as they waited patiently to enter the Grounds (bottom left)

DAY FOUR
THURSDAY 26 JUNE

When Nick Kyrgios reflects on his breakthrough year at The Championships, one of the turning points on which he is likely to dwell will be the moment when a double fault was called as he served at 5-6 and match point down in the final set against Richard Gasquet. The Australian was grateful that the second-round match was played on No.2 Court, where Hawk-Eye's all-seeing cameras enabled him to seek a second opinion. To the world No.144's relief, the result of his challenge showed that his serve was in. He went on to save what was Gasquet's fifth match point and proceeded to defend another four before completing a remarkable 3-6, 6-7(4), 6-4, 7-5, 10-8 victory. Historians could find no evidence of any man winning a match at The Championships after saving as many match points, though there is no official record of such statistics.

Nick Kyrgios raises his arms in relief after coming through in five sets against Richard Gasquet, saving nine match points in the process

At 19 years and two months Kyrgios was the youngest player in the 128-strong draw. The son of a Greek-Australian father and a Malaysian mother, he comes from Canberra, which is not renowned for producing tennis players. He was also not keen when his mother first introduced him to tennis at the age of seven, but his talent was soon evident. He won the Wimbledon boys' doubles titles in 2012 and 2013, and the boys' singles title at last year's Australian Open, which helped him become world junior No.1. Having climbed more than 600 places in the men's world rankings in 2013, he won three Challenger titles in the three months leading up to Wimbledon. After his performances at the grass court Challenger in Nottingham in early June, where he claimed the title by winning eight matches in a row, he was awarded a wild card for The Championships.

A first-round victory at Wimbledon over Stephane Robert earned a rematch with 28-year-old Gasquet, who had beaten Kyrgios in straight sets on an indoor clay court in the Davis Cup earlier in the year.

A former Wimbledon semi-finalist, Gasquet has won two of his 10 titles on grass and thus represented a formidable opponent. Everything seemed to be going to plan for the world No.14 when he won the first two sets, but Kyrgios responded well to take the third. A boisterous group of Australians, decked out in green and gold, had got behind their man from the start, and, as Kyrgios' confidence rose, so did the decibel level emanating from his supporters. He went within two points of defeat at 4-5 in the fourth set, but a break of serve in the following game helped take the match into a decider.

At 6ft 4in tall Kyrgios takes full advantage of his height to serve with impressive power. He has big ground strokes, too, but also a deftness of touch

which is demonstrated in the clever angles he finds and his fiendish drop shots. As Gasquet was soon to discover, he also has prodigious mental strength and a temperament to handle the big occasion. The Frenchman failed to convert his first three match points when he led 5-4 in the fifth set, and six more slipped from his grasp in Kyrgios' ensuing service games. At 7-7 Gasquet saved a break point with an ace, but he finally cracked two games later and Kyrgios served out for victory. The win earned the Australian a third-round meeting with the Czech Republic's Jiri Vesely, who struck another blow for the younger generation by beating Gael Monfils, one of Gasquet's fellow countrymen and contemporaries, 7-6(3), 6-3, 6-7(1), 6-7(3), 6-4.

Kyrgios was quick to acknowledge that his supporters had played a big part in his win. "I like to engage with the crowd and show a lot of emotion out there," he said. "Knowing they're going to tough it out with me for that long period really gets me going." When told that Gasquet had described him as a future Grand Slam champion and top five player, Kyrgios' response was short and to the

Rafael Nadal hops in the air after safely dispatching Lukas Rosol **(below left)**

point. "My goal is to become the No.1 player in the world," he declared.

The day's most eagerly anticipated encounter was the rematch between Rafael Nadal and Lukas Rosol, who had beaten the Spaniard at the same stage two years earlier. Nadal, who did not play for seven months after that defeat because of a knee problem, won their only subsequent meeting in Doha, but the world No.1's vulnerability on grass had been clear in the first round when he lost the first set to Martin Klizan. Struggling to handle Rosol's thunderous ground strokes, Nadal lost the first set again and went 2-4 down in the second. The match turned when Nadal hit what he called "a perfect forehand for that moment" as he faced set point at 5-6 down in a tie-break at the end of the second set. In a further twist, when Rosol served at 6-7 two points later, the world No.52 double-faulted and Nadal levelled the match, before going on to win 4-6, 7-6(6), 6-4, 6-4. Rosol

ROOF CLOSED

It took four days for the Centre Court roof to make its first appearance of The Championships, as rain fell in earnest midway through Roger Federer's second-round match against Gilles Muller. Making its slow, stately progress across the Centre Court, the roof remained shut for the rest of the match, Federer triumphing 6-3, 7-5, 6-3 under the lights at 8.30pm.

resorted to knocking over Nadal's meticulously placed water bottles in an attempt to unsettle his opponent, but early breaks in the third and fourth sets saw the 2008 and 2010 champion home.

Roger Federer and Gilles Muller, contesting the last match of the day on Centre Court, became the first players in 2014 to play under the roof after rain fell during the second set. Federer, who won 6-3, 7-5, 6-3, dropped only nine points on his serve and hit 25 aces. Meanwhile, Jo-Wilfried Tsonga, resuming against Sam Querrey after play had been suspended the previous evening at 9-9 in the deciding set, completed a 4-6, 7-6(2), 6-7(4), 6-3, 14-12 triumph, while John Isner made his latest assault on the record books. Four years

Roger Federer collects his towel during his match under the roof (above) while Heather Watson gave a good account of herself in three tough sets against Angelique Kerber (right)

to the day since he won the longest match in tennis history against Nicolas Mahut, the American won the longest tie-break at Wimbledon for 41 years in beating Jarkko Nieminen 7-6(17), 7-6(3), 7-5. The only longer tie-break was won 20-18 by Bjorn Borg against Premjit Lall in 1973.

Two of the favourites for the ladies' title maintained their impressive progress. Serena Williams, who featured in the opening match on No.1 Court after playing doubles until 9pm the previous evening, beat South Africa's Chanelle Scheepers 6-1, 6-1, taking her tally of dropped games in the first two rounds to just five. Still, that was one more game than the total lost so far by Maria Sharapova, who beat Timea Bacsinszky 6-2, 6-1. "I'm sure happy to get through an extra round than I did last year," said Sharapova, recalling her defeat to Michelle Larcher de Brito in 2013. "The first couple of matches are really crucial in just working on so many things as a grass court player, just trying to make that transition and trying to do it as quickly as possible."

The highly-thought of Eugenie Bouchard was made to work hard in the first set of her match with Spain's Silvia Soler-Espinosa, but was happy with her eventual 7-5, 6-1 victory. "It was important for me to try to close out some points at the net when I could because she was getting a few balls back," said the Canadian. "When I was stepping in and being aggressive, I felt really in control. That's always my goal."

Heather Watson, the last home representative in the ladies' singles, enjoyed the support of Niall Horan and Liam Payne, two members of the boy band One Direction, and Olympic legend Sir Steve Redgrave, but was beaten 2-6, 7-5, 1-6 by Germany's Angelique Kerber, the ninth seed. Watson lost the first set in just 26 minutes, but fought back well in the second. At 4-4 the Briton saved four break points by going for her shots as Kerber kept forcing her to play the extra ball. Watson went on to break serve

WIMBLEDON IN NUMBERS

9 The number of match points saved by Nick Kyrgios during his win over Richard Gasquet, the most saved by a player who went on to win at Wimbledon since Helga Schultze saved 11 against Janine Lieffrig in 1966.

to level the match, converting her third set point after putting Kerber in trouble with a bold backhand return. However, the No.9 seed quickly took control of the deciding set and closed out the match with impressive ease.

The most moving story of this eventful day was the return of Britain's Ross Hutchins to Wimbledon 18 months after he was diagnosed with cancer. Despite his first-round loss in the gentlemen's doubles to Pablo Cuevas and David Marrero, simply taking part was a triumph for Hutchins and his doubles partner, Colin Fleming. "This is my home club," said Hutchins. "I live three minutes away. It's great to be back having missed last year. It's the best tournament in the world. It's what you want to perform well in. We played OK, but didn't perform to our absolute best. We got outplayed a little bit today. It was a tight match, but credit to them. They played better than us."

Jo-Wilfried Tsonga (above) does a running jump after reaching the third round, while Ross Hutchins (below) returned to Wimbledon 18 months after being diagnosed with cancer

FLOWER POWER!

Head gardener Martyn Falconer stands proudly in front of the hanging baskets outside No.3 Court (above). He and his team of eight gardeners work tirelessly on all the horticulture around the Club throughout the year (right).

There is perhaps no more iconic Wimbledon flower than the purple and white petunia, situated in one of 200 hanging baskets somewhere around the All England Club's Grounds. But the 3,000 petunias, including a new red variety, were just one small part of the display of horticulture put in place for The Championships this year. A giant tennis ball (pictured right), compiled from sedum 'gold mound' and echeveria, and underplanted with hot pink petunias, greeted spectators as they lined up to watch the players at the Aorangi practice courts. Elsewhere, with Boston Ivy (*parthenocissus tricuspidata veitchii*, to be precise) adorning Centre Court and other buildings, visitors would wander past 1,100 assortments of foxgloves, lupins, hydrangeas, lavender and much more,

all designed to convey that Wimbledon is 'Tennis in an English Garden.' Not to mention over a mile of hedges (taxus, ilex and leylandii) and, of course, the world-famous Rose Arbour, featuring two varieties of rose – New Dawn and Mme Alfred Carrière.

All of this is achieved by head gardener Martyn Falconer and his team of five full-time staff, with three extra coming aboard for The Championships. They start in early April when the plants begin to arrive, and begin planting in earnest from the first week of May. That said, the flowers and plants do not just disappear post-Championships, and from July through to March, Martyn and his team spend their time maintaining the year-round seasonal displays, and making enhancements ahead of the next year's Championships.

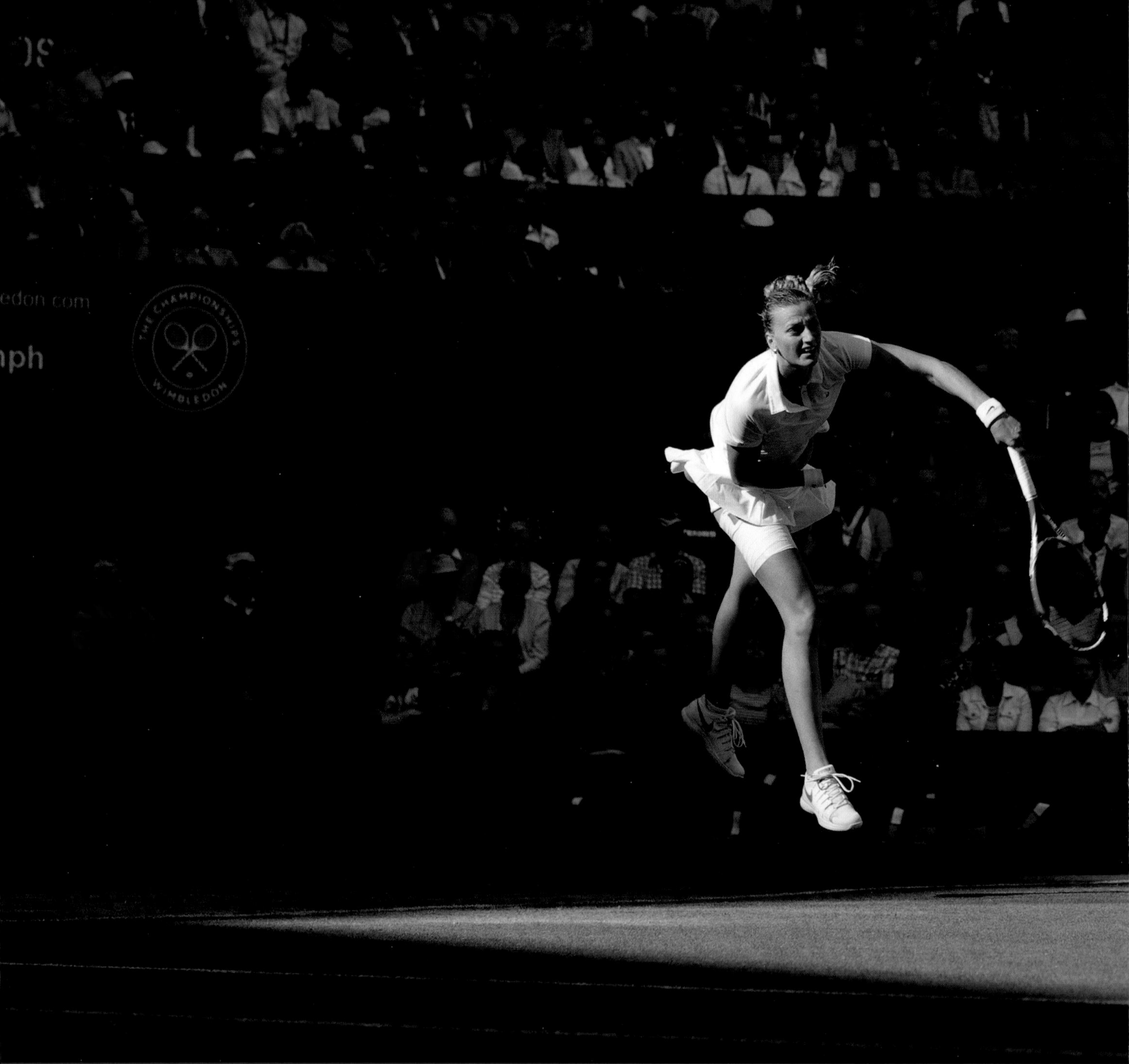
THE CHAMPIONSHIPS
WIMBLEDON

DAY FIVE
FRIDAY 27 JUNE

This was one of those days when the British weather sprung a rare but welcome surprise. Increasingly heavy rain had been predicted, possibly culminating in some thundery outbursts, but to the delight of Wimbledon watchers the forecasters got it wrong. Indeed, the weather was so clear in the evening that Tomas Berdych and Marin Cilic played to the latest finish for an outdoor match in Wimbledon history. When Cilic secured his straight-sets victory the clock on No.3 Court showed 9.38pm. Only matches under the Centre Court roof and lights have ever finished later in the day.

Tomas Berdych serves to Marin Cilic in their late-finishing encounter on No.3 Court

The afternoon programme had begun with the biggest upset of the tournament so far as Li Na, the No.2 seed, was beaten 6-7(5), 6-7(5) by the Czech Republic's Barbora Zahlavova Strycova in the opening third-round match on No.1 Court. Although Li had never gone beyond the quarter-finals at The Championships, the 32-year-old Chinese had been enjoying the best year of her career, highlighted by her triumph at the Australian Open. Zahlavova Strycova had reached the final of the Aegon Classic in Birmingham earlier in the month, but in 10 previous appearances at Wimbledon had failed to progress beyond the third round. However, it was the world No.43 who found the greater consistency, while Li made too many mistakes. Both players were broken twice in the first set, at the end of which Zahlavova

Strycova won a tightly contested tie-break. The second set was even closer: Li held her serve without too many problems, but failed to take her chances to break Zahlavova Strycova, who again edged the tie-break, despite the drama of a successful Hawk-Eye challenge by Li on match point.

The two-time Grand Slam champion blamed a lack of grass court preparation for her performance. The world No.2 did not play any competitive matches in the build-up to The Championships, having opted to miss the Aegon International at Eastbourne. "I made the wrong decision," she admitted. "I need to play some matches before the big one. It's not only about technique. I think sometimes I didn't know how to play the point, especially in the important moments. I made a lot of mistakes." Zahlavova Strycova, having reached the second week of a Grand Slam tournament for the first time in 33 attempts, put her success down to self-belief. "I thought I could do it," she said. "I feel great here and I felt great in Birmingham."

If Li was unable to find a way to play her best tennis on grass this year, the same could not be said for the two ladies who contested the second match on Centre Court. It used to be said, tongue-in-cheek, that Venus Williams had won Wimbledon so many times that the All England Club named the trophy awarded to the Ladies' Singles Champion (the Venus Rosewater Dish) after her. At the age of 34, the five-times champion is not the force she once was, but she had made it to the third round for the first time in three years. Her opponent was Petra Kvitova, the 2011 champion, who had reached the quarter-finals or better for the last four years in succession.

With their big serves, thunderous ground strokes and attacking mentality, both players are at their most dangerous on grass and the match lived up to all expectations. The best ladies' contest of the tournament so far ended in a 5-7, 7-6(2), 7-5 victory for Kvitova, with only three break points in the entire match. Williams went within two points of victory in the second set when Kvitova served at 4-5 and 15-30, but the world No.6 held on and won the tie-break to level the match. It was not until the last game of the deciding set that Kvitova finally broke Williams' serve.

Kvitova said it was the best she had played on grass since her success in 2011. Williams was disappointed to lose, but was proud of her performance and insisted that she still wanted to win Grand Slam titles. "People have been trying to retire me since I was 25," she said. "For some reason in tennis we always do that to our players. It's weird. We don't encourage them to stick around. It's like: 'Get out of here.' I'm not getting out of here. I think this year has been a great year for me."

If the defeats of Li and Williams were blows against the older generation, some of the emerging players also bowed out. Croatia's Ana Konjuh, at 16 the youngest player in the ladies' draw, was beaten 3-6, 0-6 by Caroline Wozniacki. It is 10 years since a teenager (17-year-old Maria Sharapova) won the ladies' title and Konjuh commented that she thought it would be "nearly impossible" for anyone to repeat the feat given the restrictions on the number of tournaments which younger competitors are now allowed to play.

Li Na **(top)** *saved a match point on a Hawk-Eye challenge against Barbora Zahlavova Strycova, but the Czech clinched victory at the second opportunity* **(bottom)**

France's Caroline Garcia knows all about the pressures on young players, having been singled out by Andy Murray as a future world No.1 when she pushed Sharapova hard at the French Open three years ago as a 17 year old. After losing 5-7, 3-6 to Ekaterina Makarova, Garcia admitted that it had taken time to start realising her potential. "Three years ago I couldn't play with these kind of things," she said. "It was too much stress and expectation. It took me time to grow."

Belinda Bencic, last year's girls' champion and the second youngest player in the draw at 17, reached the third round at the expense of another teenager, Victoria Duval. Simona Halep, the No.3 seed, dropped a set against Lesia Tsurenko, ranked 167 places beneath her, and remarked afterwards that she found every match on grass difficult. "You never know who will win," said the Romanian.

Berdych, the No.6 seed, became the highest ranked player to go out of the gentlemen's singles when he was beaten 6-7(5), 4-6, 6-7(6) by Cilic. When Berdych wanted to challenge a line call near the end, he was told, to his dismay, it was too dark for Hawk-Eye's cameras to operate. Cilic, the No.26 seed, confirmed that it had been "very, very dark" when the match ended at 9.38pm. To Berdych's credit, although displeased at the situation at the time, he later acknowledged that the conditions had been the same for both players and that Cilic had simply coped better.

Top seed Novak Djokovic gave his supporters a scare when he fell heavily in the third set of his 6-4, 6-2, 6-4 victory over Frenchman Gilles Simon. The world No.1 tumbled to the ground after stretching to hit a forehand and immediately clutched his left shoulder in pain. Djokovic received treatment, but when play resumed he did not appear to be in any difficulty. Having completed the third-round win, Djokovic went for an ultrasound scan. "Luckily for me it was only an impact that had a minor effect on the joint and the muscles around," he said with a palpable sense of relief. The 2011 champion's

Alexandr Dolgopolov **(left)** *threw everything his unorthodox game could muster against Grigor Dimitrov, while Novak Djokovic* **(below)** *took a painful tumble. Meanwhile, 17-year-old Belinda Bencic* **(above)** *proved why she is one to watch.*

coach, Boris Becker, always used to throw himself around the court, leading Djokovic to joke: "I talked with Boris. We obviously need to work on my diving volleys, learning how to fall down on the court. I'm not very skilful in that." Djokovic's win set up a fourth-round meeting with Jo-Wilfried Tsonga, who beat Jimmy Wang 6-2, 6-2, 7-5. At the end of the match, Tsonga gave his Wimbledon towel to a woman he had accidentally hit during the match.

WIMBLEDON IN NUMBERS

3 Number of wins Grigor Dimitrov had managed in four appearances at Wimbledon, before 2014.

Andy Murray needed just 95 minutes to beat Roberto Bautista Agut 6-2, 6-3, 6-2. The Spaniard had won a grass court title in the Netherlands in the week before The Championships, but was swept aside by an exhilarating display from the defending champion. It completed Murray's best first week at Wimbledon: his 19 games dropped was seven fewer than he conceded in his previous best year in 2010. Murray joked afterwards about the absence of his mother, Judy, who spent some of the match watching her other son, Jamie, playing in the gentlemen's doubles. "I'm obviously the No.2 son," Murray smiled. "My brother's the priority. He's the No.1 son. He's always had the preference. That's why I've been so competitive since I've been a kid."

Grigor Dimitrov, the No.11 seed, won one of the day's most entertaining matches, beating the unpredictable Ukrainian, Alexandr Dolgopolov, 6-7(3), 6-4, 2-6, 6-4, 6-1 to become the first Bulgarian man in history to reach the fourth round. Lleyton Hewitt's 16th consecutive Wimbledon ended in a 5-7, 4-6, 7-6(7), 6-4, 3-6 defeat to Poland's Jerzy Janowicz, but only after a typically whole-hearted display. It was the Australian's 42nd five-set match at a Grand Slam tournament, which beats the Open era record of 41 he had previously shared with Andre Agassi. Given Hewitt's love of competition, however, you would not bet against him finding the four additional five-set victories he needs to beat the Open era record of 29 held by Pete Sampras.

Lleyton Hewitt remains one of the experts on grass, but could not out-battle Jerzy Janowicz

GETTING AHEAD!

Come rain or shine, when you come to Wimbledon, do not forget your hat. Visitors to The Championships always bring a vast array of headgear, and 2014 was no different. From the typical McEnroe curly haired wig, to something involving strawberries and cream or tennis balls **(above and left)**, or the more practical **(below left)**, The Championships provides all manner of inspiration. Some of them, such as the creation below, surely deserve a spot in the Wimbledon Museum.

DAY SIX
SATURDAY 28 JUNE

I t was a moment of pure joy, sealed with a kiss. Having beaten Serena Williams in one of the most unexpected results of the year, Alize Cornet knelt to the ground and kissed the surface of No.1 Court. "I think it's very symbolic because it means: 'Now I love you, grass' – and I didn't before," said Cornet later in the day when asked about her celebration. "It's the best victory for me in a Slam. I made a lot of third rounds. I was really looking for this second week and now I have it. It deserved a kiss, I think."

Alize Cornet **(above)** *wearing an expression of utter disbelief after knocking out Serena Williams. She then knelt to kiss the grass she had conquered* **(right)**

One player's joy is another's despair, however, and Cornet's 1-6, 6-3, 6-4 victory was a bitter blow for Williams, who had been hoping that a return to the scene of so many of her greatest successes would revive her 2014 fortunes. The American lives for the Grand Slam tournaments and, whatever pleasure she might have derived from her title triumphs in Brisbane, Miami and Rome earlier in the year, they had not made up for her disappointments in Melbourne and Paris. After losing to Ana Ivanovic in the fourth round of the Australian Open

and to Garbine Muguruza in the second round of the French Open, a third-round defeat to Cornet, who had won only four matches in her first seven visits to Wimbledon, brought confirmation that the world No.1 is not the force she was.

Williams, five times a winner of the Ladies' Singles Championship and twice a runner-up, had lost to Cornet on a hard court in Dubai earlier in the year, but on this occasion everything appeared to be in the 32-year-old American's favour. The top seed, whose big-hitting game is made for grass, had dropped a total of just five games in beating Anna Tatishvili and Chanelle Scheepers in her first two matches, while Cornet had been taken to three sets by both Anna Karolina Schmiedlova and Petra Cetkovska. The 24-year-old Frenchwoman had won only three matches in her previous five tournaments leading up to The Championships and had recently lost to

Serena Williams was in no mood for pleasantries after the shock upset

Taylor Townsend, the world No.205, in the second round of the French Open. Nonetheless, Cornet watched video clips of her victory over Williams in Dubai to boost her confidence and went on court believing that she could win again. The world No.24 told herself that Williams was "just a human like everyone else".

However, the match had barely got under way when rain stopped play. This was a day when the weather gods wreaked their revenge after the rain forecast for the previous afternoon had failed to arrive. Only occasional showers were predicted for Saturday, but by the time the rain relented late in the afternoon more than four hours of play had been lost. When the match restarted Williams was in imperious form and reeled off five games in a row to take the first set, but then she started to falter. While mistakes began to flow from the American's racket, Cornet's confidence in her own attacking game grew. From 2-5 down in the deciding set Williams clawed her way back to 4-5, but on match point she netted a backhand after chasing down Cornet's delightful drop shot.

While Cornet's elation was evident, Williams could not wait to leave the scene of her disappointment. As Cornet sat in her chair after the match, enjoying the moment, Williams stopped behind her and tapped her on the shoulder, suggesting it was time to leave. "I think everyone in general plays the match of their lives against me," said Williams later. "Every time I step on the court I just always have to be a hundred times better. If I'm not then I'm in trouble." She added: "It's never easy being in my shoes."

Following Li Na's defeat the previous day, it was the first time in the Open era that the top two seeds in the ladies' singles failed to reach the last 16. Meanwhile, Cornet was through to the second week of a Grand Slam tournament for only the second time in 34 attempts. "If somebody would have told me a couple of years ago that I would be in the second week here at Wimbledon by beating Serena, I wouldn't have believed it," she said. "A few years ago I couldn't play on grass, I was so bad. I didn't like grass. It was just a pain to come here. I knew I would have a tough time on the court. Since last year, it's the contrary. I like coming here."

SPORTING SATURDAY

It is one of those much-loved Wimbledon traditions. On the middle Saturday of The Championships, it is the custom for the Chairman to invite those athletes who have achieved spectacular recognition for their country on the sporting scene. So it was that David Beckham **(below right)** and Sachin Tendulkar **(above left)**, two of the most famous icons in global sport, took their seats in the Royal Box to watch Rafael Nadal, Maria Sharapova and Roger Federer. According to their sports, those present in the Royal Box were as follows: From cricket, Steven Finn, Stuart Broad **(below far left)**, Phil Tufnell, Andrew Strauss and Tendulkar **(above left)**. From rugby union, England captain Chris Robshaw **(below left)**. From boxing, David Haye, Nicola Adams and Anthony Joshua **(far middle)**. From the British Winter Olympics team, Amy Williams, Lizzy Yarnold, Kelly Gallagher and Charlotte Evans **(left)**. From squash, Laura Massaro was joined by Peter Norfolk, Judy Murray and Leon Smith from the tennis world. From golf, Matthew Fitzpatrick and Ian Poulter **(below middle)**.

From swimming, Mark Foster and Tom Daley **(below left)** were joined by Matthew Pinsent from rowing. From cycling, Victoria Pendleton and Sir Bradley Wiggins **(top far left)**. From football, Sir Bobby Charlton and Beckham. And finally, in recognition of the sixth Armed Forces Day and the centenary of the First World War, representatives of the armed forces and their partners. Can you imagine the vast array of conversations?

Cornet's victory earned a meeting in the last 16 with Canada's Eugenie Bouchard, who beat her fellow French Open semi-finalist, Andrea Petkovic, 6-3, 6-4. Maria Sharapova, playing under the Centre Court roof, beat Alison Riske 6-3, 6-0, taking the number of games she had lost in her first three matches to just seven. Simona Halep beat Belinda Bencic 6-4, 6-1 to secure a fourth-round meeting with Zarina Diyas, who ended Vera Zvonareva's run. Sabine Lisicki, last year's beaten finalist, was a set up against Ana Ivanovic when play was suspended because of bad light at 1-1 in the second set.

Simona Halep muscles her way into the fourth round (above), *while Maria Sharapova played the entirety of her match under the roof* (below). *Eugenie Bouchard follows through her serve* (right)

There was high drama in the gathering gloom on Court 12, where Madison Keys, having lost the first set to Yaroslava Shvedova, took a medical time-out for treatment to her left thigh when leading 6-5 in the second set. The scoreboard was shining brightly in the darkness when play resumed at 9.31pm, but Keys appeared hardly able to walk, let alone run, and promptly dropped her serve on a double fault. With the score level at 6-6, play was finally suspended at 9.36pm due to the faltering light. Kei Nishikori and Simone Bolelli were tied at 3-3 in the final set when their third-round match was called off for the day, but Tommy Robredo completed his 6-2, 6-4, 6-7(5), 4-6, 6-3 victory over Jerzy Janowicz just in time.

It was a day when Rafael Nadal and Roger Federer were both grateful to be on Centre Court, where the retractable roof once again proved its value. Nadal's meeting with Mikhail Kukushkin followed a familiar pattern as the world No.1 won in four sets, having lost the first set for the third round in a row.

RAIN STOPS PLAY

Rain is as present at Wimbledon as the grass, and so it was little surprise when it came down in earnest on the middle Saturday to make life rather miserable for those not happily seated under the roof on Centre Court. With umbrellas unfurled on the Hill and around the Grounds, there was a steady stream of rain until the covers finally came off at 5.30pm.

WIMBLEDON IN NUMBERS

2014

The first year that two men's wild cards met in the third round of The Championships, when Nick Kyrgios took on Jiri Vesely.

Nadal found his rhythm again after the initial setback to win 6-7(4), 6-1, 6-1, 6-1 and book his place in the last 16 at Wimbledon for the first time since 2011. The Spaniard had lost to Lukas Rosol under the roof exactly two years previously and admitted later that, after losing the first set to Kukushkin, he had said to himself: "Maybe the roof here in Wimbledon is not good for me." Everything changed, however, when Nadal broke to go 3-1 up in the second set and, thereafter, the former champion's signature aggression and relentless running saw him take complete control.

Federer beat Santiago Giraldo 6-3, 6-1, 6-3 to complete his third successive straight-sets victory. "It's been a good first week for me," he said afterwards. "I've been playing well, been feeling good. I didn't drop any sets and wasn't really in danger in any of the matches." Elsewhere Milos Raonic hit 30 aces and dropped just nine points on his serve to beat Lukasz Kubot 7-6(2), 7-6(4), 6-2, while Nick Kyrgios, cheered on once again by a large group of Australian supporters, beat Jiri Vesely 3-6, 6-3, 7-5, 6-2 in a meeting of former world junior No.1s to set up a fourth-round meeting with Nadal. "I'm overwhelmed with happiness," Kyrgios said in anticipation of his meeting with the Spaniard. "It's an opportunity I'm just going to embrace."

Ball boys and girls take a break during a rain delay **(above)**, *while Tim Henman and the Wimbledon Junior Tennis Initiative juniors* **(below)** *managed their on-court display just before the heavens opened*

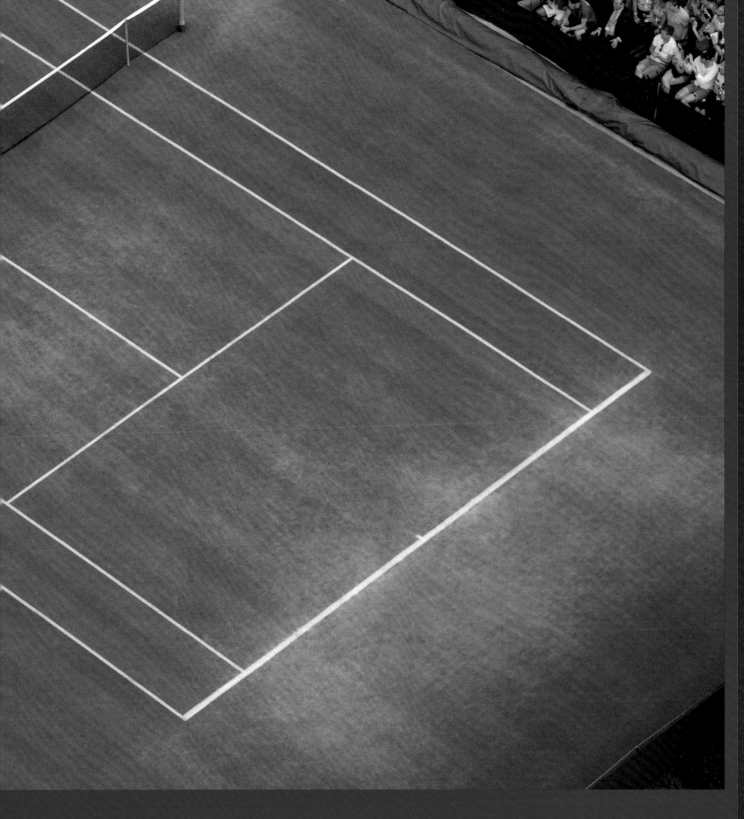

DAY SEVEN
MONDAY 30 JUNE

Andy Murray and the quarter-finals of The Championships go together like strawberries and cream, and when the Scot beat South Africa's Kevin Anderson 6-4, 6-3, 7-6(6) it was the seventh year in a row that he had reached the last eight at the All England Club. No other singles player, male or female, can match that record over the previous seven years, though Murray still has some way to go before he equals Roger Federer's sequence of 10 successive quarter-finals, a run that was ended by Sergiy Stakhovsky last year. However, even Federer's record does not match up to that of Jimmy Connors, who played in his 11th consecutive Wimbledon quarter-final in 1982.

Andy Murray reacts emphatically during his win over Kevin Anderson to reach the last eight

Much is often made of the pressure on home competitors at The Championships, but the best two British players of recent times have thrived on it. Tim Henman reached four semi-finals at Wimbledon, which was the Grand Slam event where he enjoyed the most success, and Murray has an even more impressive record. If you include the Olympic tournament in 2012, Murray's victory over Anderson was his 17th in a row at Wimbledon and his 23rd in his last 24 matches there. "I like having the nerves and I'm able to use them positively," Murray had told the world's media before his fourth-round match.

Anderson, who uses his 6ft 8in frame to deliver a huge serve, had never reached the last 16 in five previous appearances at The Championships, but was at a career-high No.18 in the world rankings. In every sense the 28-year-old South African was the biggest threat Murray had faced so far, but the defending champion took the challenge in his stride. The quality of Murray's returns negated the power of his opponent's serve, while the timing of his shot-making and the infinite variety of his game denied Anderson the chance to find any sort of rhythm. If he was not hitting precision passing shots from either flank, Murray was putting the South African in trouble with a bewitching combination of spins and slices.

Murray took the first set after breaking in the third game and was two breaks up in the second set when rain forced the players to halt proceedings while the Centre Court roof was closed. Thereafter Anderson's game picked up in the windless conditions. He played particularly well in the third set, but his only chance came and went when Murray saved a set point with an unreturned serve at 5-6 in the tie-break. After two more points the pair were shaking hands at the net. "It was a good win because he was playing very well at the end and was making it very tough for me," said Murray.

After the match Murray chatted to Sir Alex Ferguson, the former Manchester United manager, who was a guest in the Royal Box. Sir Alex, who is a big fan of Murray's, was in his player box when he won his first Grand Slam title at the US Open in 2012 and stays in regular contact with his fellow countryman, as Murray confirmed: "We send a message to each other at various times during the year."

Murray's quarter-final opponent, Grigor Dimitrov, extended his best run at The Championships by beating Argentina's Leonardo Mayer 6-4, 7-6(6), 6-2. Marin Cilic was another emphatic fourth-round winner, beating Jeremy Chardy 7-6(8), 6-4, 6-4 to set up a quarter-final confrontation with Novak Djokovic.

Djokovic's recent record of consistency across all Grand Slam tournaments is even more impressive than Murray's. In beating Jo-Wilfried Tsonga 6-3, 6-4, 7-6(5), the Serb reached his 21st Grand Slam quarter-final in succession and his sixth in a row at The Championships. Fears that the top seed might suffer some serious after-effects following the injury he sustained to his left shoulder during his third-round match were quickly allayed. "It's still a bit sore because of the fall that I had a few days ago, but there is no damage, which is important," said Djokovic. "It's normal to have a bit of soreness in the muscle and around the joint, but thankfully I have a flexible shoulder, and it helps in these particular situations."

Kevin Anderson at full stretch as he tries to disrupt Murray's rhythm

Two days after bad light thwarted his attempt to finish off Simone Bolelli in the third round, Kei Nishikori completed a 3-6, 6-3, 4-6, 7-6(4), 6-4 victory. Stan Wawrinka, whose third-round match had not even started on Saturday, beat Denis Istomin 6-3, 6-3, 6-4 to earn a fourth-round meeting with Feliciano Lopez, who beat John Isner 6-7(8), 7-6(6), 7-6(3), 7-5. With Isner going out and Madison Keys unable to complete her match against Yaroslava Shvedova because of a thigh injury, the United States were left without a representative in the fourth round of either the gentlemen's or the ladies' singles for the first time since 1911.

Shvedova's reward for beating Keys was a fourth-round meeting with Sabine Lisicki, who beat Ana Ivanovic 6-4, 3-6, 6-1 to win a third match in a row for the first time during an injury ravaged year. The match resumed at 1-1 in the second set after play had been suspended on Saturday night because of limited light, though there was another interruption when rain began to fall on No.1 Court towards the end of the second set. Ivanovic, who over the last year has enjoyed her best run since her victory at the French Open in 2008, took advantage of a dip in Lisicki's form to take the second set, but the German quickly resumed control in the decider. After the match Lisicki conveyed her appreciation for the support she received from the public. "The crowd knows my story here," the 2013 runner-up said. "I came here as a young girl and I came back from injury. It's a big story with Wimbledon. I love the support that I'm getting here."

Barbora Zahlavova Strycova, who had knocked out Elena Vesnina and Li Na in her two previous matches, defeated a seeded player for the third round in a row to reach her first Wimbledon quarter-final. The world No.43 beat Caroline Wozniacki 6-2, 7-5 to secure a meeting with her fellow Czech, Petra Kvitova, the 2011 champion, who beat China's Peng Shuai 6-3, 6-2. Ekaterina Makarova proved too strong for Agnieszka Radwanska, overwhelming the 2012 runner-up 6-3, 6-0 to book a quarter-final berth against Lucie Safarova, who beat another Czech, Tereza Smitkova, 6-0, 6-2.

As is often the case, Alize Cornet, who had provided the shock result of the ladies' singles so far by knocking out Serena Williams 48 hours earlier, could not sustain her momentum and was beaten 6-7(5), 5-7 in the

Japan's Kei Nishikori is swamped by fans **(above left)**, *while Barbora Zahlavova Strycova* **(below)** *beat Caroline Wozniacki to reach her first Wimbledon quarter-final*

AN OPEN AND SHUT CASE

Wimbledon's Centre Court roof has more than proved its worth in the five years since it was unveiled in 2009. The retractable roof, which weighs 1,000 tonnes and spans 5,200 square metres, is deployed 'at the discretion of the referee' and has been used to avoid interruption from impending rain, and to allow a match to be finished due to failing light. But, all that said, Wimbledon remains an outdoor, daytime event. And so, while there was some confusion during the second Monday when the Centre Court roof remained open, despite impending rain being forecast, the referee's decision did allow for an hour and a half of the break in showers to be played in outdoor conditions. "They should always try to play with the roof open because it's an outdoor event," said Andy Murray when asked why the roof had been open for the start of his fourth-round match against Kevin Anderson. "I think we need

to give the players the opportunity to play outdoors as long as possible. When it does rain and you know it's going to be there for a while, they obviously need to close it. But we played for, what, 1 hour and 20 minutes or 30 minutes outdoors. It wasn't like it was just five or ten minutes."

By 2019, The Championships will also have a retractable roof on No.1 Court, which will allow for uninterrupted tennis for a combined total of over 26,000 people.

WIMBLEDON IN NUMBERS

1911

The last time that no American reached the fourth round at Wimbledon. John Isner's third-round loss to Feliciano Lopez sealed the 103-year-old stat.

opening match on Centre Court by Eugenie Bouchard, who remained on course for a third successive appearance in a Grand Slam semi-final. "Every match I play, I believe I can win," said Bouchard. "I've proved to myself I can play on the big stage. I've played on centre courts of most of the Slams."

With the Countess of Wessex among the guests in the Royal Box, the media were keen to know more about Bouchard's interest in the royal family, the 20-year-old Canadian and her twin sister, Beatrice, having been named after princesses. Asked if she had "princess-like tendencies," Bouchard admitted with a smile: "I can be a princess. I can be moody in the morning. I'm not so much of a morning person. My fitness trainer carries my tennis bag around. But that's so I don't get tired because I want to save all my energy for the match. I can demand a few things once in a while – but I do it with love."

Lucie Safarova (above) advanced to her first Wimbledon quarter-final, as did Eugenie Bouchard (below)

QUALIFIED SUCCESS!

Qualifying for The Championships is an underrated task. A total of 128 men and women gather on the grass courts of the Bank of England Sports' Grounds, a brief drive from the All England Club grounds, to begin their quest to earn one of 16 elusive spots in the main draw. Qualifiers have to win three matches on grass, back-to-back, against a combination of experienced foes and up-and-comers. It can be where young stars come to the fore, such as American Victoria Duval or Anett Kontaveit of Estonia. It can be where elders of the game try for one last hurrah, such as former semi-finalist Gilles Muller. It can also be where British hopes gain valuable world-class exposure. And, by the time

they reach the main draw first round, qualifiers can be a banana skin for their opponents, having had three matches to hone their grass court game. Among those to peform as such, advancing all the way to the fourth round of The Championships, was Tereza Smitkova of the Czech Republic **(pictured above)**. The 19-year-old, making her Wimbledon debut, took three sets to beat American Madison Brengle in the final round of qualifying, before going on to upset Su-Wei Hsieh in the first round, and finally succumbing to compatriot Lucie Safarova in the fourth round. The most successful of the men's qualifiers was Jimmy Wang, who reached the third round, before losing to Jo-Wilfried Tsonga.

Tereza Smitkova of the Czech Republic during her successful passage from qualifying to the main draw

DAY EIGHT
TUESDAY 1 JULY

It is a good job that Centre Court is built on solid foundations because you could have sworn that the ground had shaken. Nick Kyrgios' victory over Rafael Nadal was not only the biggest upset of this Wimbledon Fortnight, but also one of the greatest shocks in the 137-year history of The Championships. Nadal, the world No.1, twice a champion at the All England Club and the holder of 14 Grand Slam titles, was beaten 6-7(5), 7-5, 6-7(5), 3-6 by a 19-year-old Australian making his Centre Court debut.

Nick Kyrgios jumps for joy during his upset of Rafael Nadal

Kyrgios, the world No.144, became the first male player ranked outside the top 100 to beat a world No.1 since Andrei Olhovskiy defeated Jim Courier in the third round of The Championships in 1992. He was also the first teenager to defeat a world No.1 at a Grand Slam tournament since Nadal knocked Roger Federer out of the 2005 French Open, and the lowest ranked player ever to beat Nadal at a Grand Slam tournament.

Yet even those astonishing facts barely convey the magnitude of Kyrgios' achievement. Courier had never gone beyond the quarter-finals at Wimbledon when he suffered his 1992 meltdown, while Nadal was world No.5 and already had a victory over Federer under his belt when they met at Roland Garros in 2005. A more telling comparison would be Pete Sampras' defeat to a 19-year-old Federer in the fourth round at Wimbledon in 2001, which ended the American's attempt to win the title for an eighth time, or Boris Becker's storming of The Championships in 1985 when the German won his first All England Club title at the age of 17.

There was certainly something Becker-like in Kyrgios' performance. Fuelled by the boldness of youth, the 6ft 4in Australian hit 37 aces and 70 winners, and one of his winning shots was a stroke of breathtaking impudence. Caught flat-footed by a baseline shot, he played a half-volley between his legs which flew over the net and took Nadal completely by surprise. There was only one break of serve apiece, but, crucially, Kyrgios served better in the tie-breaks. "I was not able to read his serve during the whole match," conceded Nadal afterwards.

It was not as if Nadal played badly. The Spaniard's vulnerability had been evident in his first three matches, when he lost the first set on each occasion, but the common consensus was that his level would rise in the second week. Even Kyrgios' mother gave her son no chance. "She thought Rafa was too good for me," Kyrgios revealed after the match. "It actually made me a bit angry." Asked what he would say when he next spoke to her, Kyrgios said: "I'll just text her a smiley face." The young Australian had undoubtedly experienced the best week of his career so far, but insisted he was "just a normal 19-year-old kid". He added: "I play a lot of Xbox. I brought my Xbox with me. Never did I think a week ago that I was going to make the quarter-finals of Wimbledon in my first appearance."

John McEnroe declared that Kyrgios had the look of a man who thought he could go on to win the title, but the teenager said that he was determined to "stay grounded". Perhaps he had in mind the example of another Australian teenager who reached the quarter-finals when ranked outside the world's top 100. Bernard Tomic, who was 18 when he made the last eight in 2011, has struggled to realise his potential ever since.

It was Nadal's third successive Wimbledon exit at the hands of lowly ranked opponents, following his defeats to Lukas Rosol (world No.100) in 2012 and Steve Darcis (world No.135) in 2013. "On this surface, when you have an opponent who decides to serve and to hit every ball very hard, you are in trouble," said Nadal. He added with a smile: "Congratulations to him. For me, beach."

Kyrgios' reward for beating Nadal was a quarter-final meeting with Milos Raonic, who celebrated Canada Day by overpowering Kei Nishikori 4-6, 6-1, 7-6(4), 6-3. Raonic, who hit 35 aces, became only the second Canadian man to reach the quarter-finals at The Championships, following in the footsteps of Robert Powell, who last achieved the feat in 1912. Eugenie Bouchard, who beat Raonic into the last eight by 24 hours, is the only other Canadian to have made the quarter-finals.

Roger Federer and Stan Wawrinka both won delayed fourth-round matches to set up an all-Swiss quarter-final. Federer had lost to Tommy Robredo at last year's US Open, but needed only 94 minutes to conquer his fellow 32-year-old 6-1, 6-4, 6-4. Meanwhile, on No.2 Court Wawrinka beat another Spaniard, Feliciano Lopez, 7-6(5), 7-6(7), 6-3.

The ladies' quarter-finals featured an all-Czech affair, with Petra Kvitova beating Barbora Zahlavova Strycova 6-1, 7-5. Zahlavova Strycova had no answer to Kvitova's power in the opening set and missed her chance of getting back into the match when she failed to serve out for the second set when 5-4 ahead. Kvitova's reward was a semi-final meeting with another Czech, Lucie Safarova, who beat Ekaterina Makarova 6-3, 6-1. It was the first time in the Open era that three Czechs had reached the quarter-finals of a Grand Slam tournament simultaneously.

Rafael Nadal reacts in anguish (**below**) *as he fails to disrupt Kyrgios' rhythm* (**above**)

A NEW STAR IS BORN!

With a collective age of 381 years and a bulging cabinet of 38 Grand Slam singles trophies between them, you might think that Rod Laver, Ashley Cooper, Ken Rosewall, Neale Fraser and John Newcombe might like to re-live past glories and fond memories when gathered together at Wimbledon. But no, the five Australian legends of the game, assembled for a press conference, wanted to talk about Nick Kyrgios.

"It's absolutely fantastic – probably the best result from an Australian player in 20 or 30, maybe 40 years," said former world No.1 Fraser. "It shows we have a player who's the real deal." Laver agreed: "I saw him earlier this year in Melbourne and he seemed raw, bombing away, hitting big shots, not always going in. But against Rafa, on Centre Court, he

didn't have nerves. He has confidence in his ability. And 37 aces! If you serve well, you play well." And Cooper chipped in: "He reminded me of Boris Becker, who came from nowhere and actually won the tournament. Or Sampras at the US Open in 1990." The future is very bright for Australian tennis.

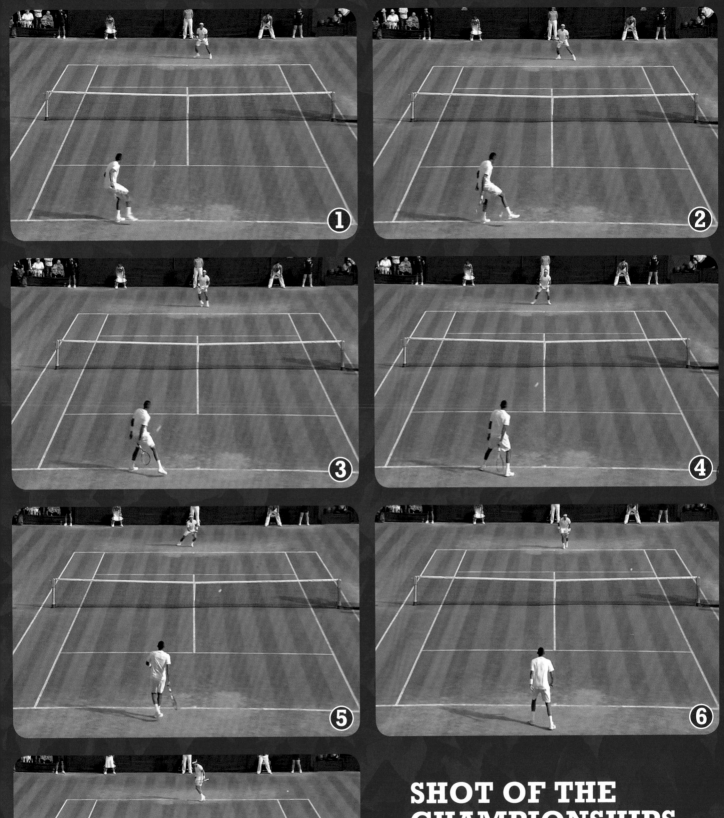

SHOT OF THE CHAMPIONSHIPS

It was as if he was standing in his back yard at home in Australia, not on Centre Court facing Rafael Nadal. Leading Nadal by one set to love, at 3-3 in the second set, 40-0 on Nadal's serve, Kyrgios, running back into the middle of the court, chose to hit his forehand between his legs, but played the shot so casually that he almost did not realise he had done it. Nor did Nadal. The shot floated over the net, leaving the Spaniard stumped. It was the most-watched video of The Championships.

WIMBLEDON IN NUMBERS

100

Number of tie-breaks by day seven, the first time the number of tie-breaks at any Grand Slam has reached triple figures.

Maria Sharapova's hopes of winning a second Wimbledon title 10 years after her first were ended when she was beaten 6-7(4), 6-4, 4-6 in a delayed fourth-round match by Angelique Kerber. Sharapova struck the ball with great power throughout, but in Kerber she met a player who loves making her opponent hit the extra ball. The German led for most of the first set, recovered from a slow start in the tie-break and then responded well after losing the second set. The No.9 seed went 5-2 up in the decider, only for Sharapova to fight back in typical fashion. The Russian saved a match point in the eighth game and then broke to trail 4-5. Sharapova went 0-40 down in the following game and saved five more match points until her resistance finally crumbled as Kerber went on the attack.

"She's never really a player that gives you a lot of mistakes," said Sharapova afterwards. "You really have to win the match against her." Asked if she was tired following her French Open victory and run at Wimbledon, Sharapova said: "I think I've actually had a really rejuvenating trip, to be honest. I know it's been very physical and I played a lot of matches." Kerber admitted that she had got nervous towards the end. "I was trying to focus just from point to point," she said. "I was telling myself: 'You can do it. She will not make mistakes. If you want to win the match, you need to be aggressive, just go for it.' And I did that. I'm happy that I actually won the match. I think she didn't lose the match. I won it. That feels good."

The 2013 runner-up Sabine Lisicki, despite requiring extensive treatment on a sore shoulder, emerged victorious from her clash with Yaroslava Shvedova 6-3, 3-6, 6-4. The No. 19 seed took a medical time-out early in the third set and needed further treatment during changeovers. The injury meant that she was unable to serve with her usual power, but she gritted her teeth to secure her quarter-final place against Simona Halep, who beat Kazakhstan's Zarina Diyas 6-3, 6-0. "I wasn't able to lift my arm," admitted Lisicki. "I was serving at 50 miles an hour or something. I don't remember if I ever served that slow in my life before."

While there were shockwaves in the girls' singles and mixed doubles events, as top seeds Ivana Jorovic and Catherine Cartan Bellis were beaten by Paula Badosa Gibert and Maia Lumsden respectively, and Mike Bryan and Katarina Srebotnik lost to Chris Guccione and Oksana Kalashnikova, the strangest events of the day took place on No.1 Court. In a bizarre and worrying series of events, the Williams sisters' campaign in the Ladies' doubles ended in distressing scenes. Serena felt unwell during the warm-up against Kristina Barrois and Stefanie Voegele, and only started the second-round match after lengthy discussions with the doctor. She did not look herself, however, and hit four successive double faults in the third game, with her serves either barely reaching the net or ballooning way over it. Kader Nouni, the umpire, came on court to speak to her and at the end of the game the sisters retired to sympathetic applause. The reason for Serena's withdrawal was later disclosed to be a viral illness.

Serena Williams receives medical attention after worrying signs during the warm-up for her doubles match with sister Venus

CZECH IT OUT

The Czech Republic is no stranger to success on the Grand Slam stage, but Wimbledon 2014 provided a new record for the home of Martina Navratilova, the most successful Wimbledon singles champion in history. Petra Kvitova, Lucie Safarova and Barbora Zahlavova Strycova had all advanced to the quarter-finals, making the Czech Republic the best-represented nation in the last eight of the singles, and the best their country had ever performed at Wimbledon. Led by Kvitova, the twice-recent Fed Cup champions advanced fearlessly; Kvitova defeated compatriot Zahlavova Strycova (playing her first major quarter-final), while Safarova out-hit Russian Ekaterina Makarova to set up an all-Czech semi-final.

"We have a lot of good players, even in [the] top 100. Tennis has a huge tradition in the Czech Republic," explained Safarova. "It's a very popular sport and we are used to changing surfaces, because in the winter we are playing indoors." "It kind of makes you adapt to different surfaces and we are usually players who are playing really fast and aggressive. So that's the key to how to play on grass well, so I think it fits."

Lucie Safarova (above), Barbora Zahlavova Strycova and Petra Kvitova (below) show their delight at reaching the quarter-finals

WIMBLEDON FROM THE AIR

'Tennis in an English Garden' – that is the mantra of The Championships. And when viewed from above, SW19 looks exactly like that. Reams of green grass courts, with the spectators moving seamlessly between them, are decorated with flowers, brown benches and clean green tarps, making Wimbledon one of the most unique sites in the sporting world.

DAY NINE
WEDNESDAY 2 JULY

Winning Wimbledon for the first time is hard enough, but it seems that defending the title is an even greater challenge. Since Boris Becker won his second successive All England Club title 28 years ago, Pete Sampras and Roger Federer are the only men who have successfully defended their trophies 12 months after their maiden victories. When Andy Murray's attempt to retain his 2013 crown ended in a 1-6, 6-7(4), 2-6 defeat to Grigor Dimitrov, he was at least in good company. Novak Djokovic, Andre Agassi, Stefan Edberg and Pat Cash are among those who have tried and failed to defend their first Wimbledon titles.

Andy Murray shows his frustration during a below-par performance

Given Murray's difficulties in the last 12 months, ranging from back surgery to a parting of the ways with his former coach, Ivan Lendl, the fact that he lost in the quarter-finals was hardly unexpected. What was surprising, however, was the manner and margin of defeat, especially after he had not dropped a set in the tournament so far and had played some sparkling tennis in his first four matches.

Dimitrov, the world No.13, was the first player ranked outside the world's top 10 to beat Murray at Wimbledon since 2006. Furthermore, the defeat ended Murray's 17-match winning streak, if you include the Olympic tournament in 2012, and his quest for a sixth consecutive semi-final at the All England Club.

Murray looked out of sorts from the start of his seventh successive Wimbledon quarter-final. Normally one of the quickest players around the court, he often failed to get into position to play his shots. The errors multiplied and his second serve regularly came under attack. "As soon as we started warming up I sensed his game was not at his highest level," said Dimitrov afterwards. "I've practised quite a few times with him. I know how he's striking the ball when he's at his best. I know how he's playing when he's not at his best. It was just a feeling that I had."

When the match got under way, an emboldened Dimitrov hit some huge returns, attacked the net when the opportunity arose and played some splendid volleys in a fine display of aggressive grass court tennis. "He was the better player from start to finish," admitted Murray. "I made many unforced errors and then started going for too much and taking chances that weren't really there."

Murray had a break point in the opening game, but thereafter he struggled. Dimitrov took the first set in just 25 minutes and held firm after Murray retrieved a break midway through the second. In the third set the Scot double-faulted when serving at 2-3 and break point down. At 2-5 another double fault gave Dimitrov two match points, the second of which the Bulgarian converted when Murray netted a forehand. The crowd had been subdued for much of the match as the home hero laboured, but rose to acclaim both men as they left the court. Before they did so, Murray had the presence of mind to remind Dimitrov to bow to the Royal Box, where the Duke and Duchess of Cambridge, the Duke of Kent and Princess Beatrice were among those present.

After suffering his heaviest defeat at Wimbledon for six years, Murray promised to work "harder than ever". He also revealed that after The Championships he would discuss his future coaching plans with Amelie Mauresmo, who worked with him on a trial basis during the grass court season. "I need to go away and make a lot of improvements in my game," said Murray. "I need to have a think about what

Meanwhile, Grigor Dimitrov produced one of the matches of his career

are the things I need to improve and get myself in better shape and work even harder, because everyone's starting to get better."

Dimitrov had never previously beaten a top 10 player at a Grand Slam event. "It's a great feeling," he said. "It's something that I've worked for – to get on to that stage, come out, and switch to another gear. It's a quarter-final match, playing against the defending champion, against a gentleman like Andy. That adds a lot. At the same time, it's just another match for me. I'm happy I'm through in three sets." The Bulgarian was asked what tips his girlfriend, Maria Sharapova, had given him. He replied: "She says: 'Win it.' What can I say? I think that's a good tip."

FIT FOR A KING

From left to right:
All England Club
President HRH
The Duke of Kent,
All England Club
Chairman Philip
Brook, HRH The
Duchess and
HRH The Duke of
Cambridge, and
Mrs Brook in the
Royal Box

It is known as one of the most prestigious seats in sport. The All England Club's Royal Box, where patrons, members and invited guests have taken their place to watch the events during The Championships since 1922, has a deserved reputation. The Royal Box has 74 seats, in the shape of dark green Lloyd Loom wicker chairs (pictured below). Invitations come from the Chairman of the All England Club, and guests are invited to the Clubhouse for lunch, tea and drinks. Among those invited are members of the British and Overseas Royal Families, heads of government, commercial partners, supporters of tennis and other walks of life. Those invited to the Royal Box this year included the Duchess of Cornwall, the

Duke of York, the Duke and Duchess of Cambridge, Princess Eugenie, Sir Richard Branson, Shaquille O'Neal, Hugh Jackman, David Beckham, Sir Bruce Forsyth, Sir Cliff Richard, Larry Ellison, Samuel L. Jackson, Keira Knightley, Jude Law, Colin Firth, Sir Michael Parkinson and many more.

The recently refurbished Clubhouse drawing room and Members' Balcony (top), and a selection of images from the Members' Dining Room, including the Royal Box pins for guests (far right)

Novak Djokovic **(above)** *takes a tumble during his five-set win over Marin Cilic*

Milos Raonic **(below)** *celebrates, while Roger Federer* **(below right)** *consoles Stan Wawrinka*

While Dimitrov was winning on Centre Court, his semi-final opponent, Novak Djokovic, was on No.1 Court recording his 10th successive victory over Marin Cilic. Djokovic, who won 6-1, 3-6, 6-7(4), 6-2, 6-2, admitted that he had been distracted by the noise coming from Centre Court. "I said to the chair umpire: 'Let's just stop the match, put it live on the big screen, and let's watch it till they're done. It's going to be better for all of us'."

The No.1 seed, who struggled with his footing until he changed into a new pair of shoes early in the fourth set, conceded that he had not dictated the pace of the match enough but was pleased with his durability. "I thought that Marin got a little bit tired physically," said Djokovic. "I was looking at him in the fourth set. He wasn't moving as well any more, so I tried to get him from one corner to another, to mix up the pace. I've done pretty well in the last two sets."

In the following match on No.1 Court, Nick Kyrgios' unforgettable run ended with a 7-6(4), 2-6, 4-6, 6-7(4) defeat to Milos Raonic, who became the first Canadian to reach the semi-finals since 1908. Raonic hit 39 aces and dropped his serve only once, with Kyrgios admitting he had "nothing left" following his quarter-final triumph over Rafael Nadal.

The victory sent Raonic into a semi-final showdown with Roger Federer, who won his all-Swiss meeting with Stan Wawrinka. Dropping a set for the first time in the Fortnight, Federer won 3-6, 7-6(5), 6-4, 6-4. "He was hitting it so well, so I had to wait for my chance," said Federer after completing his 14th win in 16 meetings with his Davis Cup colleague. "It's hard against a friend because we know each other's game so well." Wawrinka, whose third-round match had been delayed until Monday because of

bad weather, said it had been tough to play three days in a row, "especially when you played the third against Roger".

Earning a place in his ninth Wimbledon semi-final was particularly satisfying for Federer after his experience 12 months ago, when he lost in the second round to Sergiy Stakhovsky. "Last year was rough," said Federer. "It was a major disappointment for me because I always see Wimbledon as one of my main goals of the season."

WIMBLEDON IN NUMBERS

35 Grand Slam singles semi-finals reached by Roger Federer out of 61 Grand Slams played

Romania's Simona Halep and Canada's Eugenie Bouchard set up an intriguing semi-final clash as they became the first players from their respective countries to reach the last four of the ladies' singles. Bouchard beat Angelique Kerber 6-3, 6-4, while Halep won 11 games in a row to beat Sabine Lisicki, last year's runner-up, 6-4, 6-0.

Bouchard, the 2012 junior champion, reached her third successive Grand Slam semi-final after an impressively resolute performance. There were no breaks of serve until the world No.13 went 5-3 up in the first set, but she took immediate command of the second by building a 4-1 lead. Kerber admitted she had struggled to recover following her momentous victory over Sharapova the previous day. At this time last year, Halep had not gone beyond the second round of a Grand Slam event, but her latest victory took her within one win of a second successive final after she finished runner-up to Sharapova at the French Open. "I feel more confidence at the Grand Slams now," said Halep. "I can play better and better. I just want to be happy, to be relaxed."

Su-Wei Hsieh and Peng Shuai, the defending champions and No.1 seeds in the ladies' doubles, were beaten 6-4, 6-7(5), 2-6 by Timea Babos and Kristina Mladenovic. In the mixed doubles Belinda Bencic came up against Martina Hingis, her childhood idol and the daughter of her coach, Melanie Molitor. Hingis and Bruno Soares beat Bencic and Martin Klizan 6-3, 5-7, 9-7 to reach the quarter-finals.

Simona Halep (below left) celebrates a comprehensive victory over last year's runner-up Sabine Lisicki (below)

DAY TEN

THURSDAY 3 JULY

On the hottest day of the British summer so far, at least two spectators fainted through heat exhaustion, though Eugenie Bouchard and Petra Kvitova kept their cool to book their places in the ladies' singles final. Bouchard, playing in only her sixth Grand Slam tournament, albeit in her third successive major semi-final, beat Simona Halep 7-6(5), 6-2 to become the first Canadian to reach a Grand Slam final. Meanwhile Kvitova, the 2011 champion, defeated Lucie Safarova 7-6(6), 6-1 in the first ladies' Grand Slam semi-final to be contested by two Czechs.

Eugenie Bouchard and Simona Halep do battle (above), *while Halep receives treatment on her left ankle* (right)

Bouchard's consistent excellence in 2014 made it easy to forget her youth and inexperience. The 20-year-old Canadian, who was the youngest player in the world's top 20, did not play her first senior Grand Slam event until the French Open in 2013 and was world No.66 when she appeared at The Championships last summer. She broke into the top 20 after making the semi-finals at the Australian Open in January 2014, and it was only with her quarter-final victory at Wimbledon that she secured a place in the top 10.

On the other side of the net on Centre Court, Halep had made similarly spectacular progress during the past year. The 22-year-old Romanian arrived at the All England Club having won seven titles in the previous 13 months – more than any woman other than Serena Williams – and fresh from her first appearance in a Grand Slam final, having finished runner-up at the French Open to Maria Sharapova. Now she was attempting to become the first Romanian to reach a Wimbledon singles final since Ilie Nastase in 1976.

However, the world No.3 went into the semi-final suffering from muscle pain and her chances took a further turn for the worse after only four games when she twisted her left ankle and required a medical time-out. "I felt a big pain," said Halep afterwards. "It was better after it was taped, but I still couldn't push on my leg any more. My first serve was really bad after that."

Nevertheless the first set went to a tie-break, though there was a further interruption when Kader Nouni, the umpire, stopped play after spotting that a spectator had fainted. "It's pretty tough to stop in the middle of a tie-break," said Bouchard later. "It was intense, and then to just not play tennis for three minutes messes up the rhythm. But I took it as a challenge. I was like: 'OK, this is the same for both of us. This is happening. I'll just go out and try my best'."

Bouchard drew level at 4-4 in the tie-break thanks to a lucky net cord and went on to take the set. Looking deflated, Halep was soon down 1-5 in the second set and had to save three match points to hold her serve for 2-5, one of them with an ace which Bouchard felt should not have counted because she had raised her hand following a shout from the crowd. However, the Canadian kept her composure to complete victory in the following game.

A picture of calm assurance throughout, Bouchard was asked afterwards: "Do you ever go nuts?" She replied: "I'm waiting for a big moment to go nuts. Of course, achieving a lifelong dream like winning a Slam would be very exciting to me, but I feel like my job is not done here, so there's no need for a huge celebration because I'm still working. I still have another match."

Eugenie Bouchard's composure in reaching her first Grand Slam final was admirable

Bouchard said that winning the Wimbledon junior title two years previously had helped her when she joined the main tour. "It definitely gave me confidence," she said. "I think the transition after winning the juniors was definitely a big point in my career. It's helped me since then, not just at this tournament, but of course I feel extra special here, a little bit like I'm at home. It's always enjoyable coming to Wimbledon."

The Canadian was also unsurprised to reach her first Grand Slam final. "I expect good results like this," she said. "I was like: 'OK, good. It's a step in the right direction. I get to play in the final.' I still have another match, so it's not a full celebration yet." She added: "I've been believing since the beginning of the tournament that I can do really well. I'm just trying to take it one match at a time. It's really important not to get ahead of ourselves, but I totally feel like I belong. I'm just so excited for the next match."

In the all-Czech ladies' semi-final, Kvitova held the head-to-head advantage after having won all five of her previous meetings with Safarova, though her friend and Fed Cup colleague had run her close the previous month at Eastbourne before losing in a final set tie-break. Safarova, making her Grand Slam semi-final and Centre Court debut, was broken in the opening game but levelled at 2-2. The two left-handers both struck the ball with great power and matched each other until Kvitova edged the tie-break. Her confidence rising, Kvitova then took immediate control of the second set, which she won in just 29 minutes. Gracious in defeat, Safarova offered the warmest of congratulations. "Petra is my friend," she said. "I just wished her all the best. I hope she's going to win it."

SCORCHING SUMMER

The sunshine came out in earnest for Ladies' semi-finals day as a packed Centre Court watched Eugenie Bouchard and Simona Halep. It was later agreed to be the match of the day.

A spectator receives medical attention in the heat

Kvitova admitted that there had been times since winning the Ladies' Singles Championship in 2011 when she had struggled. "I've been really up and down over these three years," she said. "I knew that a lot of people were expecting something more from me, but on the other hand I was still in the top 10 and I did everything I could. I was practising very hard, but it's never easy. There were a lot of positive things, but when I won here in 2011 I definitely needed to change myself a little bit on and off the court to cope with the pressure, the media and everything like that."

She added: "It's difficult to handle the pressure every time you step on the court. Most of the time you are the favourite and it's not easy. It takes time to get used to that. That's something I am living with right now. I don't think it can change. It's part of my life right now."

Over on Court 12, Safarova suffered her second defeat of the day in the quarter-finals of the ladies' doubles when she and her partner, Anastasia Pavlyuchenkova, were beaten 1-6, 6-4, 3-6 by Zheng Jie and Andrea Hlavackova, whose next opponents, Sara Errani and Roberta Vinci, emerged victorious over last year's runners-up, Casey Dellacqua and Ashleigh Barty, 6-4, 2-6, 6-0. Timea Babos and Kristina Mladenovic beat Alla Kudryavtseva and Anastasia Rodionova 6-3, 3-6, 6-4 to secure a semi-final meeting with Andrea Petkovic and Magdalena Rybarikova.

Wimbledon crowd favourites Leander Paes and Radek Stepanek reached the semi-finals of the men's doubles, overcoming Daniel Nestor and Nenad Zimonjic 3-6, 7-6 (5), 6-3, 6-4. The competitors played under the intense summer sun and, as a result, the match was halted early in the first set when Paes alerted the umpire after noticing that a spectator, the second of the day, had fainted in the heat. Vasek Pospisil and Jack Sock, the only unseeded pair in the last eight, beat No.2 seeds Alexander Peya and Bruno Soares 6-4, 3-6, 7-6(6), 6-4.

Twenty-four hours after Andy Murray lost on Centre Court, his brother Jamie won there in the mixed doubles alongside Dellacqua, the Scot and the Australian beating Horia Tecau and Sania Mirza 7-5, 6-3. The British pair Neal Skupski and Naomi Broady also reached the quarter-finals, conquering Florin Mergea and Elina Svitolina 4-6, 6-3, 6-4, though they needed 11 match points to complete their victory. Skupski was so overcome by the victory that, attempting to throw a ball into the crowd, he inadvertently sent it back over his own head instead.

WIMBLEDON IN NUMBERS

885 Aces hit during the ladies' singles tournament by the end of the semi-final stage, a substantial increase from 752 in 2013

In the boys' singles, Tim Van Rijthoven of the Netherlands caused the biggest upset so far by defeating Russia's Andrey Rublev, the No.1 seed, 7-6(6), 4-6, 7-5 to secure a quarter-final meeting with Noah Rubin, a product of the John McEnroe Tennis Academy in New York. The unseeded Rubin had knocked out the No.7 seed, Francis Tiafoe, 7-6(4), 4-6, 6-3. In the girls' singles, Tornado Alicia Black, the highest seed remaining, beat Britain's Katie Boulter 6-1, 6-2 to advance to the quarters.

(Far left) Petra Kvitova smiles as compatriot Lucie Safarova congratulates her on her victory (Below) Jamie Murray and Casey Dellacqua on their way to the quarter-finals of the Mixed Doubles

DAY ELEVEN
FRIDAY 4 JULY

			ROLEX		1.50
3.01					
PREVIOUS SETS				SETS GAMES POINTS	
6 3	Novak DJOKOVIC			1 5 30	
	v				
4 6	Grigor DIMITROV			1 4 40	
CHALLENGES REMAINING					
N. DJOKOVIC	2				
G. DIMITROV	3				

t had been the talk of the Wimbledon Fortnight, but now it was time for actions to speak louder than words. If the new wave of younger players was about to take over at the top of the men's game, here was a golden opportunity to demonstrate that the times were indeed changing. The Championships had produced a semi-final line-up in the gentlemen's singles that encapsulated the power struggle taking place within the sport.

Grigor Dimitrov and Novak Djokovic face each other from the turf after giving every last ounce during an engaging rally

Both matches brought together one of the four players who had dominated for the best part of a decade and one of the young pretenders. Roger Federer, the winner of a record 17 Grand Slam titles, faced 23-year-old Milos Raonic, whose big-hitting game made him arguably the most dangerous of the new guard. The other semi-final opposed Novak Djokovic, the No.1 seed and winner of six Grand Slam titles, and another 23-year-old, Grigor Dimitrov, perhaps the most stylish of the newly emerging generation.

Until the start of 2014, the 'Big Four' of Federer, Djokovic, Rafael Nadal and Andy Murray had won 34 of the previous 35 Grand Slam tournaments. However, Stan Wawrinka's victory at the Australian Open in January 2014 had fuelled talk of changes at the top, even if the 28-year-old Swiss was more old guard than new wave. Nevertheless, the established order was back in place at the French Open, where Nadal beat Djokovic in the final and Murray joined them in the semi-final line-up.

The domination of the four men has left few opportunities for other players to sample even a taste of competition at the business end of Grand Slam tournaments. While Federer was playing in his 35th Grand Slam semi-final and Djokovic in his 23rd, neither Raonic nor Dimitrov had ever been to such a stage before. Raonic, a Canadian, and Dimitrov, a Bulgarian, were also aiming to break new ground for their countries, neither of which had ever produced a Grand Slam finalist. For all their inexperience, however, there could be no doubting their talent. Raonic was at a career-high No.9 in the world rankings, while Dimitrov had won four titles in the previous nine months, most recently at The Queen's Club in the build-up to The Championships.

While it would be wrong to describe the two semi-finals as an anti-climax – the quality of the tennis was much too high for that – the battle of the generations was a more one-sided contest than many had expected. While Djokovic was pushed hard by Dimitrov before securing a 6-4, 3-6, 7-6(2), 7-6(7) victory, there was an air of inevitability about the outcome of the second semi-final on Centre Court. It was almost as if some of Raonic's self-belief had drained away in the wake of Dimitrov's defeat. Federer won 6-4, 6-4, 6-4 to ensure that the Big Four would maintain their grip on the game's greatest honours.

Djokovic, playing in his 16th semi-final in the last 17 Grand Slam tournaments and in his fifth in a row at The Championships, asserted his authority from the start. Dimitrov had attacked Murray's second serve to great effect in his previous match, but Djokovic immediately put 19 first serves in succession into court and took the first set in just 27 minutes. Dimitrov struggled to find his timing and had trouble with the sun when serving at one end on a gloriously warm afternoon, while both the Bulgarian and the Serb had difficulty keeping their feet on the worn areas of grass behind the baselines. Djokovic resorted to changing his shoes midway through the third set.

When Djokovic broke serve in the third game of the second set, Dimitrov looked to be in deep trouble, but the world No.13 responded in admirable fashion, breaking serve twice in a row to take the second set. At 2-4 in the third set tie-break, however, Dimitrov double-faulted, then put an attempted drop shot in the net and, finally, failed to return a serve. Nevertheless, the Bulgarian had his chances in the fourth set. Djokovic saved one set point when he served at 4-5, and three more after Dimitrov went 6-3 up in the tie-break, before sealing victory on his second match point with a forehand cross-court winner.

Djokovic admitted there had been times in the match when he had shown his frustrations when his level had dipped. "As the final stages of a Grand Slam are coming to you, of course the tension and expectations and the pressure rise," he said. "I'm a perfectionist on the court. I want things to go a proper way from the first to the last point, so sometimes I get carried away with emotions." Dimitrov regretted his slow start, but said he would take positives from his first Grand Slam semi-final. "I think I got my act together and I was really playing good tennis," he said. "You never know what would have happened if I had taken that fourth set."

In the second semi-final, Raonic knew he would have to serve well to have any chance of winning, but got off to the worst possible start as a double fault helped Federer break in the opening game. Federer had dropped his own serve only once in his first five matches and on this occasion offered just one break point, which he saved in the eighth game of the first set. Raonic, who hit 17 aces to take his total at The Championships to 164, the highest tally of the tournament, generally held serve without too much difficulty, but crumbled again at 4-4 in both the second and third sets. A double fault and a missed smash contributed to the break in the second set, and a missed forehand in the third gave Federer the chance to serve out for victory. Amongst those in the Royal Box who must have been suitably impressed were Rod Laver, the only man to win all four Grand Slam tournaments in the same year on two occasions, and Jack Nicklaus, the winner of a record 18 major golf championships.

Maria Sharapova (top) watches Grigor Dimitrov from his player box while Boris Becker (bottom) urges on his charge Novak Djokovic

It was a match of twists, turns and angles as both Novak Djokovic **(above)** and Grigor Dimitrov **(right)** stretched every sinew during their semi-final. But it was Djokovic who prevailed with a roar **(far right)**

(overleaf) Seven-times champion Roger Federer proved too masterful for Milos Raonic, playing in his first Wimbledon semi-final

ROLEX
0.25
FEDERER 4 0
v
Milos RAONIC
CHALLENGES REMAINING
FEDERER 2
RAONIC 2

WIMBLEDON IN NUMBERS

164
Aces served by Milos Raonic during his six matches at Wimbledon 2014, the most of the tournament

Raonic said he had expected to play much better and hoped he would learn from the experience in future. Asked what he would most like to do now that his tournament was over, Raonic smiled. "Eat unhealthy," he said. "Right now I'm craving chicken wings."

Federer's delight in reaching his ninth Wimbledon final, extending his own all-time record, was evident. "My game's back where I hoped it would be from one year ago," he said afterwards. "Things were difficult for most of last year. I'm happy I worked hard off the court to get myself back into shape and back into contention for tournaments. This year's been very solid. I've reached a lot of semis and finals." Did Federer think that talk of a changing of the guard had been premature? "It was always going to be hard to get rid of all four guys at the same time," he said. "It was probably inevitable there would be one guy around, maybe two."

Raonic's fellow Canadian, Vasek Pospisil, earned a place in the gentlemen's doubles final alongside his American partner, Jack Sock, the scratch pairing beating the highly experienced Leander Paes and Radek Stepanek 7-6(5), 6-3, 6-4. Bob and Mike Bryan reached their 11th Wimbledon final by beating Michael Llodra and Nicolas Mahut 7-6(4), 6-3, 6-2. Timea Babos and Kristina Mladenovic, who were friends and doubles partners as juniors, beat Andrea Petkovic and Magdalena Rybarikova 6-1, 6-3 to reach the final of the ladies' doubles. Sara Errani and Roberta Vinci, the No.2 seeds, reached their first Wimbledon final with a 6-3, 6-2 victory over Andrea Hlavackova and Zheng Jie.

Pakistan's Aisam-Ul-Haq Qureshi and his Russian partner, Vera Dushevina, booked a place in the mixed doubles semi-finals against Nenad Zimonjic and Samantha Stosur by beating Britain's Neal Skupski and Naomi Broady 6-4, 6-3. Max Mirnyi and Hao-Ching Chan beat Jamie Murray and Casey Dellacqua 6-2, 3-6, 6-3 to set up a semi-final meeting with Daniel Nestor and Kristina Mladenovic.

Three teenagers from the United States reached the last four of the boys' singles. Taylor Harry Fritz and Noah Rubin were both unseeded, while Stefan Kozlov, the No.6 seed, earned a semi-final meeting with France's Johan Sebastien Tatlot, the No.8 seed. Tornado Alicia Black, at No.3 the highest remaining seed in the girls' singles, was beaten 3-6, 1-6 by Jelena Ostapenko in the quarter-finals. Ostapenko's quick-fire victory earned a semi-final against Marketa Vondrousova, while Kristina Schmiedlova, the No.8 seed, would meet Elena Gabriela Ruse to complete the final four.

Roger Federer acknowledges the reception from the Centre Court crowd after advancing to his ninth Wimbledon final

HELLO CANADA

It will be a Wimbledon to remember for Canadian tennis. The sport in Canada is more commonly associated with rich country club folk, so for Eugenie Bouchard, Milos Raonic and Vasek Pospisil to give tennis a leg-up in a nation known for its love of ice hockey is certainly something worth talking about.

"I don't have a huge sense of [the excitement in Canada] because I'm across an ocean and in my own kind of bubble," said Bouchard. "I'm not really reading anything or caring too much about the outside talk. I just hope they're proud of me. When I go back home, I'll be excited to go back to Canada."

Where Bouchard's rise has been relatively swift, going from junior champion in 2012 to ladies' finalist in 2014, Raonic's has been more measured. The 23 year old broke through to reach his first major fourth round at the Australian Open in 2011, but has stuttered since. Wimbledon's grass has proved to be the perfect fillip.

Meanwhile, Pospisil, the world No.33 and the surprise package in Canada's run to the Davis Cup semi-finals in 2013, is optimistic that there is more to come. "I think if the children here in Canada can see the Canadian players having good results, it can only be positive for tennis in Canada," he said. "I really hope this will continue, and that tennis will be able to become a major sport in Canada in the future."

Milos Raonic (above), Vasek Pospisil and Eugenie Bouchard (below) put Canada firmly on the tennis map this Wimbledon

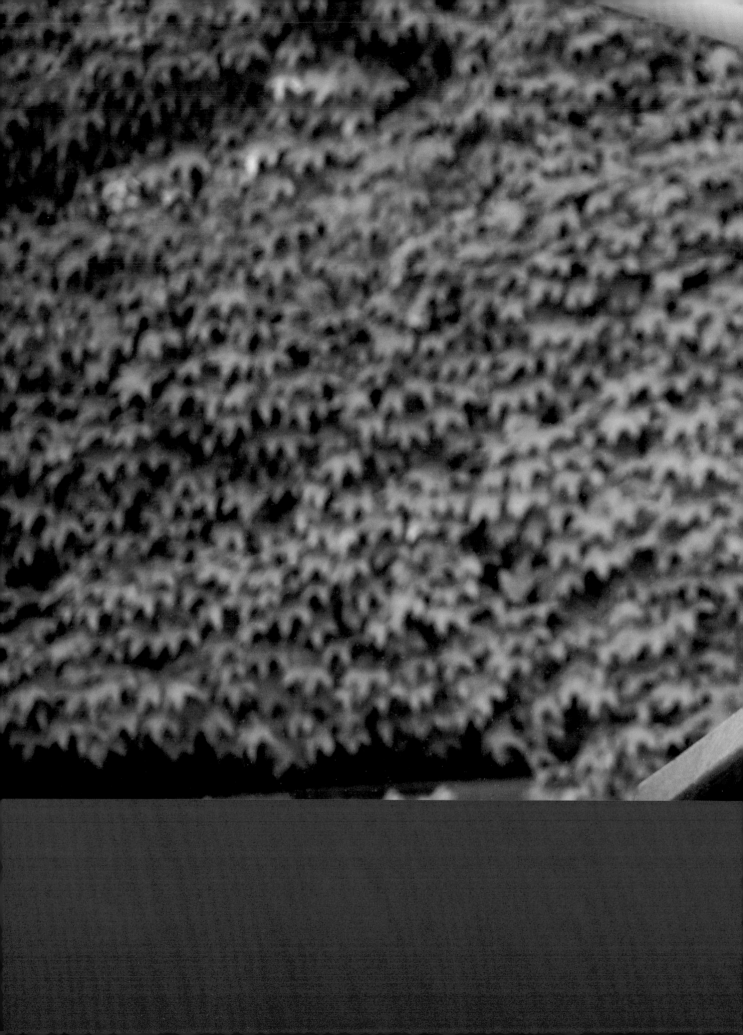

DAY TWELVE
SATURDAY 5 JULY

I f the final of the gentlemen's singles was to oppose two of the four men who had dominated the sport for the best part of a decade, the ladies' singles final was more of a vision of the future, even if it did feature a returning champion in Petra Kvitova. The 24-year-old Czech, who won the title in 2011, and 20-year-old Eugenie Bouchard, who won the girls' title the following year, contested the first Grand Slam singles final between two players who had been born in the 1990s. Indeed, Kvitova was the only player born in the 1990s who had won a Grand Slam singles title.

Petra Kvitova and Eugenie Bouchard walk down the stairs from the locker room before walking out onto Centre Court for the ladies' singles final

The continuing success of older players has not been as significant in the women's game as it has in the men's, but it has nevertheless been a noticeable trend. Serena Williams, who became world No.1 for the sixth time last year at the age of 31, was the oldest woman in tennis history to top the rankings, while Li Na, Samantha Stosur, Francesca Schiavone and Marion Bartoli had all won their maiden Grand Slam titles at comparatively late stages in their careers. With the game becoming more physical and with restrictions on the number of tournaments that teenagers can play, the chances of anyone repeating Maria Sharapova's 2004 feat of winning Wimbledon at the age of just 17 appear to be receding with every year.

The combined age of the finalists this time was 44 years and 239 days, which made it the youngest Grand Slam final since 20-year-old Ana Ivanovic faced 22-year-old Dinara Safina at the 2008 French Open. Bouchard in particular was a comparative novice, even though she had reached the semi-finals of the 2014 Australian and French Opens. The first Canadian ever to reach a Grand Slam singles final, she was playing in only her sixth senior Grand Slam competition. In the Open era, Chris Evert is the only woman to have reached her first Wimbledon final having played fewer Grand Slam events.

Kvitova might have seemed like an old hand in comparison, but that was because she had won here three years previously at the age of just 21. The big-hitting left-hander has experienced her ups and downs since then. Although a regular contender in the latter stages of subsequent Grand Slam events, she had failed to reach another final. She admitted that coping with the attention that had followed her Wimbledon triumph had not been easy.

Given the excellence of both players' tennis in their first six matches, a high-quality final was expected. What had not been anticipated, however, was a brutally one-sided contest as Kvitova poured on the power in one of the best performances seen in a final for many a year. The Czech won 6-3, 6-0 in just 55 minutes as Bouchard was swept away by wave after wave of bold attacking strokes. The world No. 13 was never given time to settle as Kvitova recorded the quickest victory in a ladies' singles final at the All

England Club since Martina Navratilova, her fellow Czech, beat Andrea Jaeger by the same scoreline in 54 minutes in 1983. Navratilova looked on admiringly from the Royal Box alongside a number of other former champions, including Maria Bueno, Martina Hingis, Virginia Wade and Bartoli. Princess Eugenie, after whom Bouchard's mother had named her, was also in the Royal Box, while the Canadian had plenty of supporters among the public, who had taken her to their hearts over the Fortnight.

The coin toss was carried out by 15-year-old Medina Djouada, who was representing the European Association for the advancement of research into Leukodystrophies, a group of genetic disorders generally diagnosed in childhood, which, as is the custom, was the charity nominated by 2013 champion, Marion Bartoli.

From left to right: Petra Kvitova, Chair Umpire Marija Cicak, 15-year-old Medina Djouada, Eugenie Bouchard and Referee Andrew Jarrett pose for the coin toss. Medina was representing the European Association for the advancement of research into Leukodystrophies

The ladies' final began under dark and stormy clouds

It was the performance of a lifetime from Petra Kvitova, who blistered her way to her second Wimbledon title with tennis of such quality that Eugenie Bouchard, her opponent, had no say in the matter. Kvitova was dominant throughout, her serve a particularly devastating factor, and her joy in victory was evident for all to see

STAIRWAY TO HEAVEN

Petra Kvitova (above) hugs her coach David Kotyza in her players' box after winning her second Wimbledon title. She entered the box through the newly created gate (right)

The very first Wimbledon champion to perform the now-famous climb to his player box was Pat Cash in 1987, leaping over the commentary box as he did so. Rafael Nadal did the same in 2008, even going one step further by clambering over to the Royal Box to shake hands with the Spanish crown prince. And Andy Murray, of course, did so in memorable fashion after winning both Olympic gold and the Wimbledon men's singles title on Centre Court. This year, the powers-that-be at the Club decided to make the climb a little easier for those to perform, and avoid any risk of broken ankles or otherwise, by creating a set of steps and a Champions' Gate into the box. When asked if the new gate had spoiled

the 'tradition', Maria Sharapova said, beautifully clearly, "I heard you can open the gate. Gates open." So it was that Petra Kvitova became the first champion to use the gate, embracing her team happily after her scintillating victory.

It had rained in the morning but the weather cleared in time for the start of the match, although it was still overcast and considerably cooler than it had been in recent days. What colour was lacking in the skies, however, was rapidly replaced by the brightness of Kvitova's play. The Czech's booming ground-strokes, struck with little top spin but great accuracy, zipped off the grass, denying Bouchard the time to strike the ball effectively. With Kvitova also serving sweetly, the prospects for Bouchard quickly looked ominous. Unlike Sabine Lisicki 12 months earlier, the Canadian did not show any signs of nerves, but never got into the match.

Kvitova broke serve in the third game with a thumping forehand cross-court winner and performed the same feat again in the seventh game. Bouchard, to her credit, broke back, but a third break of serve gave Kvitova the first set. The Czech took her game up yet another level in the second set and it was soon a question of whether Bouchard would get on the scoreboard again. She did not and Kvitova completed her victory in appropriate fashion with a thunderous backhand cross-court winner.

Petra Kvitova poses for photographs with the Venus Rosewater Dish for the second time in her career

The weather's timing was almost as good as Kvitova's. Once the new champion had celebrated with her team, the players left the court briefly while the roof was closed because rain was about to fall. The short break gave Bouchard a moment to reflect on her experience. "I was in the engraver's room, so I was watching them work, wishing one day, dreaming that he'll write my name somewhere," she said afterwards, almost wistfully.

Despite the pain of losing in a Grand Slam final, Bouchard paid tribute to Kvitova. "She played unbelievably and didn't give me many opportunities to stay in the rallies," said the Canadian. "She's

WIMBLEDON IN NUMBERS

28 Winners produced by Petra Kvitova in her 55-minute victory, which equates to just over one every two minutes.

been playing well all tournament and was really going for it today. I didn't feel like I was able to play my game. She really took the chances away from me and was really putting a lot of pressure on me. I didn't have that many opportunities. Sometimes your opponent just plays better than you."

Kvitova agreed that she had played one of the matches of her career. "I knew that I could play well on the grass," she said. "I knew exactly what I had to do to beat her. I was very focused on every point. I knew that I had to go forward with every shot to push her."

In contrast, Bouchard's fellow Canadian, Vasek Pospisil, enjoyed a remarkable victory in the men's doubles final alongside his American partner, Jack Sock. In their very first event as a team, Pospisil and Sock beat the veteran American twins Bob and Mike Bryan 7-6(5), 6-7 (3), 6-4, 3-6, 7-5. The Bryans have won a record 15 Grand Slam doubles titles, including three at Wimbledon. Asked what the secret was in beating them, Pospisil said: "Close your eyes and hope you play the best tennis of your life."

In the ladies' doubles final, Sara Errani and Roberta Vinci added the one trophy missing from their Grand Slam collection when they beat Timea Babos and Kristina Mladenovic 6-1, 6-3. Playing in their first final at the All England Club, they became the first ladies' pair to win all four Grand Slam titles since Venus and Serena Williams did so in 2001. They are also the first Italians to ever win a senior Wimbledon title, their unrivalled joy conveyed in what was the celebration of The Championships.

Mladenovic suffered further disappointment in the mixed doubles. She and Daniel Nestor, were beaten 7-6(4), 7-5 in the semi-finals by Max Mirnyi and Hao-Ching Chan. Nenad Zimonjic and Samantha Stosur won the other semi-final, beating Aisam-Ul-Haq Qureshi and Vera Dushevina 7-5, 6-2.

Stefan Kozlov, aged 16, earned his second appearance in a junior Grand Slam final this year when he won his semi-final in the boys' event, beating France's Johan Sebastien Tatlot 6-3, 7-6(7). Tatlot was the

Petra Kvitova proudly holds the Venus Rosewater Dish on the Members' Balcony as spectators gather, umbrellas in tow, to congratulate her

only non-American to make it to the last four. In the other semi-final, Noah Rubin beat Taylor Harry Fritz 6-4, 6-2. Rubin was leading 6-4, 5-1 when play was suspended because of rain, but did not need long to complete his victory once the match had resumed. The semi-finals of the girls' singles were won by Kristina Schmiedlova, the No.8 seed, and the unseeded Jelena Ostapenko. Schmiedlova, from Slovakia, beat Romania's Elena Gabriela Ruse 4-6, 6-3, 6-4. Schmiedlova led 2-0 in the second set when rain stopped play and quickly got on top when play restarted. Ostapenko had a much more straightforward victory, the Latvian eliminating Marketa Vondrousova, of the Czech Republic, 6-1, 6-2 in just 48 minutes. The stage was set for the final day.

ROLEX 0.56

	SETS	GAMES	POINTS
Timea BABOS Kristina MLADENOVIC	0	3	30
V			
Sara ERRANI Roberta VINCI	1	5	4

CHALLENGES REMAINING

T. BABOS / K. MLADENOVIC	1
S. ERRANI / R. VINCI	2

AND THERE'S MORE!

Petra Kvitova was not the only champion of the day. Roberta Vinci and Sara Errani **(above)** produced some of the photos of the tournament after beating Timea Babos and Kristina Mladenovic to win the ladies' doubles title and complete their career Grand Slam, before Vasek Pospisil and Jack Sock **(left)** set about creating one of the upsets of the tournament, defeating the Bryan brothers to win the men's doubles title.

DAY THIRTEEN
SUNDAY 6 JULY

The weather gods smiled on The Championships in 2014. The Centre Court roof may have had to roll into action on several occasions and bad weather on the middle Saturday caused some disruption to the programme in the second week, but for the most part the sun shone and play was uninterrupted. The weather was especially kind on the last day, when the morning rain cleared by lunchtime to leave a beautiful English summer's afternoon. It returned only in mid-evening, by which time most spectators were on their way home and the guests at the Champions' Dinner were heading for the Royal Opera House.

Roger Federer, Chair Umpire James Keothavong, Referee Andrew Jarrett and Novak Djokovic look on as 12-year-old Nathan Bullimore performs the coin toss. **(Right)** *The Duke and Duchess of Cambridge, and Samuel L. Jackson, watch from the Royal Box*

For the ninth time in 12 years the final of the gentlemen's singles featured the player widely acknowledged as the greatest of all time. Roger Federer was hoping to add to his numerous records and become the first man to win eight Wimbledon singles titles and, at 32 years and 332 days, the oldest to win in the Open era, the record having been set by Arthur Ashe at 31 years and 360 days in 1975. Federer already held the record for the most appearances in the final (this would be his ninth), the most Grand Slam men's singles titles (17) and the most consecutive appearances in Grand Slam events (59).

Djokovic's career statistics may not match up to Federer's, but in almost any other era they would be exceptional. Victory here would give the Serb his seventh Grand Slam singles title, which would put him in joint eighth place on the Open era list alongside John McEnroe and Mats Wilander. At 27 years and 45 days he was the fourth youngest man in the Open era – after

Bjorn Borg, Rafael Nadal and Federer – to reach 14 Grand Slam singles finals. Nevertheless, a recent record of five defeats in his last six Grand Slam finals had been a cause of concern for Djokovic, who had recruited Boris Becker to his coaching team in an attempt to improve his record in the final stages of the biggest events. Becker's opposite number in Federer's player box was Stefan Edberg, thus renewing the great rivalry between the German and the Swede that had lit up Wimbledon a quarter of a century previously.

Coincidentally, Becker and Edberg met 35 times during their careers, which was the exact number of meetings Djokovic and Federer would reach in this year's final. The Swiss led their head-to-head record by 18 wins to 16, though many of their matches had been desperately close, including two successive US Open semi-finals which Djokovic won 7-5 in the final set after saving two match points. This was their 12th meeting at a Grand Slam tournament, equalling the record set by the equally fierce rivalry between Djokovic and Nadal. Federer had won in four sets in their only previous meeting at Wimbledon, in the 2012 semi-finals, and had won their only previous encounter in a Grand Slam final, at the US Open in 2007.

The build-up to the first Grand Slam final for four and a half years not to feature Nadal or Andy Murray promised a great match – and that was exactly what the two men provided. Djokovic produced one of the performances of his life to win 6-7(7), 6-4, 7-6(4), 5-7, 6-4 after nearly four hours of unrelenting drama. Federer saved a match point in the fourth set, which he won from 2-5 down, and appeared to have the upper hand when Djokovic sent for the trainer because of a leg problem early in the decider, but the Serb showed great character to claim his second Wimbledon title.

The quality of the tennis was exceptional. The number of winners (143) dwarfed the number of unforced errors (56) and there were many magnificent rallies as both men demonstrated their athleticism by hitting great shots off balls that most others would have failed to reach. Federer in particular served superbly, hitting 29 aces. Djokovic's instinct is to counter-punch, but under Becker's guidance he showed a greater willingness to move forward. Meanwhile, Edberg had finessed Federer's attacking game by encouraging him to use more slice and to hit more balls down the middle, cutting down on his opponents' opportunities to pass.

BECKER VS EDBERG

A rivalry was revived as Boris Becker and Stefan Edberg faced off in a Wimbledon final on Centre Court for the fourth time in their careers. Except, of course, neither was playing. Becker was seated sternly, and at times exuberantly, in Novak Djokovic's player box, while Edberg sat serenely in Roger Federer's. The last time they had met on Centre Court, Edberg triumphed in five sets in the 1990 final. Becker led their head-to-head 25-10, but Edberg won two of their three finals at Wimbledon. Who would win No.4?

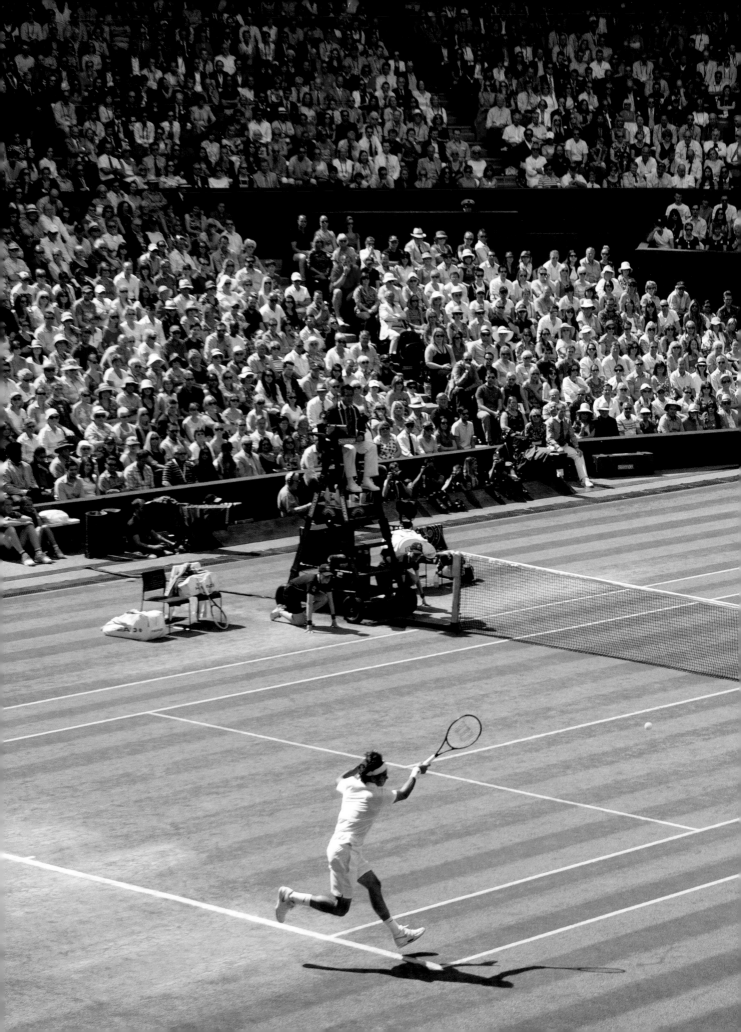

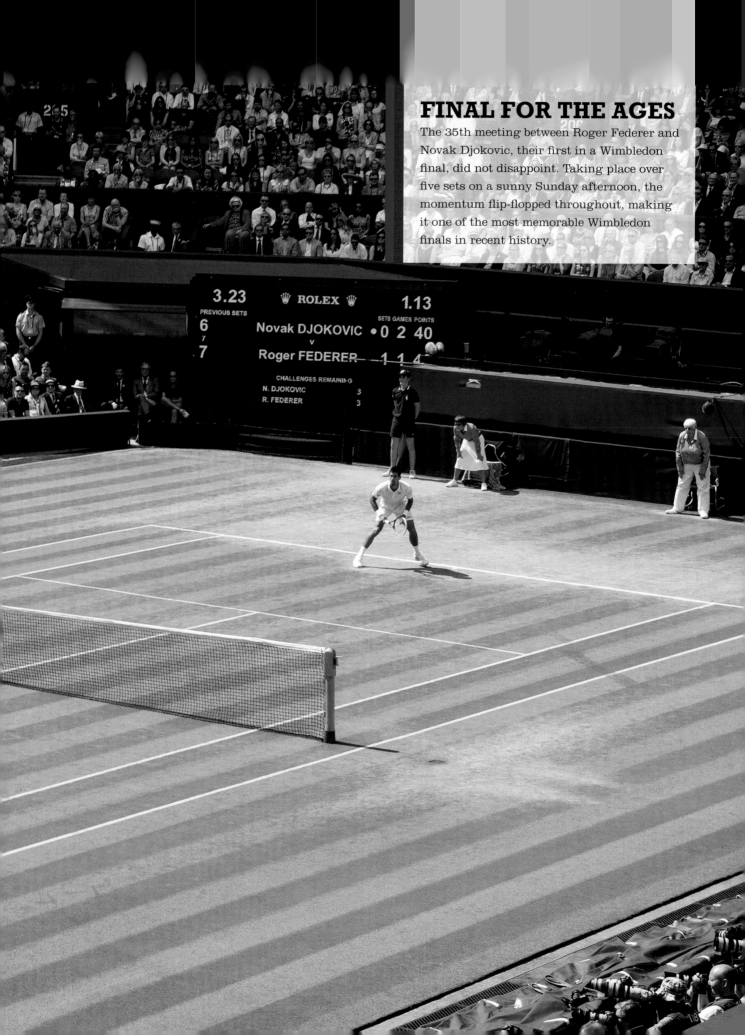

FINAL FOR THE AGES

The 35th meeting between Roger Federer and Novak Djokovic, their first in a Wimbledon final, did not disappoint. Taking place over five sets on a sunny Sunday afternoon, the momentum flip-flopped throughout, making it one of the most memorable Wimbledon finals in recent history.

The coin toss was performed by Nathan Bullimore on behalf of Action for Children Scotland, the charity nominated by Murray, the 2013 champion. The host nation was also represented in the umpire's chair as James Keothavong, elder brother of former British No.1 Anne, took charge of his first Grand Slam final.

It was quickly clear that the majority of the crowd were behind Federer, even though Djokovic had Britain's favourite German on his side. Neverthless, the No.1 seed made the better start, dropping only two points in his first four service games and pushing Federer hard on his. By the end of the first set both men were playing beautifully. Federer led 3-0 and 4-2 in the tie-break, but had to save two set points before winning three points in a row from 6-7 down to take the set.

An early break for Djokovic – the first of the match – secured the second set, in the last game of which the Serb had to defend a break point for the first time. There were no breaks of serve in the third set. At 4-4 Federer played the perfect game, winning it with four successive aces, but he was forced to save two break points two games later. The set went to another tie-break, but this time Djokovic took an early lead before converting his first set point when Federer put a backhand wide.

Djokovic seemed to be in control when he broke to lead 3-1 in the fourth set, only for Federer to break back immediately to a huge roar from the crowd. Among those who stood to applaud was the actress Kate Winslet, who presumably knows a titanic struggle when she sees one. However, Djokovic broke again and went 5-2 up, only to fail to serve out for the set, to even louder appreciation from the crowd. At 4-5 Federer saved a Championship point with an ace, for which he was grateful to Hawk-Eye after

Novak Djokovic dives in trademark fashion to keep the ball in play

the ball had been called out. Djokovic, with nerves apparently getting the better of him, played a poor game to drop serve again at 5-5, after which Federer served out the set by winning his fifth game in a row. With chants of "Roger! Roger!" bouncing around the stadium, the momentum was now clearly with the Swiss veteran.

As Djokovic sent for the trainer to treat a leg problem early in the deciding set, statisticians started to research the last time that the final had been won by a player who had saved a Championship point. The answer was Bob Falkenburg in 1948. At 3-3, with Federer pressing hard, Djokovic saved a break point, but in the following game the Swiss had to save three, the last of them with a sensational half-volley. Two games later, however, with Federer serving at 4-5, Djokovic forced two Championship points, requiring only one of them as Federer netted a backhand.

Having thrown his arms in the air, Djokovic knelt down and ate a blade or two of the Centre Court grass – without even checking whether it was gluten-free. Asked afterwards what it had tasted like, he replied: "It tasted like the best meal I have ever had in my life."

After Djokovic had celebrated with his entourage, the crowd rose to acclaim Federer as he collected his runner-up trophy. Among those applauding were his twin daughters, Charlene and Myla, who had joined their mother in his player box. "You know it's going to be tough facing him [Djokovic]," Federer told the crowd. "I can only say congratulations: an amazing match, an amazing tournament, and deserved, well deserved."

Roger Federer shows his intent after battling back into the match

Djokovic, who struggled to hold back the tears, said that Wimbledon was "the tournament I always dreamed of winning – the best in the world". He added: "It was a great match to be part of. Roger is a great role model and a great champion and I thank him for letting me win today."

Djokovic replaced Nadal at the top of the world rankings with his victory, but, more importantly, this was the day when the Serb regained his self-belief after a run of losses in Grand Slam finals. Federer's initial disappointment at the result was evident, but here was proof that, given full fitness, he remains a contender for the biggest prizes. Retirement is not on his agenda. "That clearly makes me believe that this was just a stepping stone to many more great things in the future," he said.

At the Champions' Dinner in the evening, Djokovic was still on top form. "My brother is writing on his phone not listening, but he knows what I'm going to say," the Serb joked at the start of his speech. He said his thoughts would now turn to his forthcoming wedding to Jelena Ristic. "My priority from tomorrow onwards is to remember what flowers go on what table," he said. Earlier Petra Kvitova, the ladies' champion, had told the guests how her run to the title had been fuelled by the cooking of her racket stringer, who prepared a regular meal of pineapple and rice for her. This led Djokovic, who was set to become a father later in the year, to joke: "I'm going to ask Petra for her stringer's phone number

Novak Djokovic savoured his moment of victory, raising his arms in the air, tasting the grass, and letting the emotion overwhelm him **(facing page)**. *He then proceeded to his players' box to celebrate with his team* **(above)**, *before the trophy presentation* **(below)**

WIMBLEDON IN NUMBERS

35

The number of meetings between Roger Federer and Novak Djokovic. Their coaches, Boris Becker and Stefan Edberg, had also met 35 times.

because we will have an extra mouth to feed next year. I like the sound of her pineapple and rice."

The other finals played on the last day of the Fortnight were equally captivating. Noah Rubin beat his fellow American, Stefan Kozlov, 6-4, 4-6, 6-3 to win an excellent boys' singles final on No.1 Court. Rubin, aged 18, had to win eight matches to take the title after coming through qualifying. "The atmosphere was unbelievable," he said afterwards. "I didn't expect [the court] to be that packed." Latvia's Jelena Ostapenko won the girls' title, recovering from a set down to beat Slovakia's Kristina Schmiedlova 2-6, 6-3, 6-0. When reminded that Eugenie Bouchard had won the title two years previously, 17-year-old Ostapenko said: "I think I have to maybe follow her and try to do the same. I will try my best."

Britain's Jordanne Whiley and Japan's Yui Kamiji won the wheelchair ladies' doubles title by beating Jiske Griffioen and Aniek Van Koot 2-6, 6-2, 7-5, and the victory was even sweeter as Whiley and Kamiji had lost to the same opponents in the previous year's final. Stephane Houdet and Shingo Kunieda retained the wheelchair gentlemen's doubles title, beating Maikel Scheffers and Ronald Vink 5-7, 6-0, 6-3.

The Championships ended in traditional fashion on Centre Court with the mixed doubles final, which was won by Australia's Samantha Stosur and Serbia's Nenad Zimonjic, who beat Chan Hao-Ching and Max Mirnyi 6-4, 6-2. It was Stosur's second Wimbledon mixed doubles title and Zimonjic's first, though the Serb had previously won mixed doubles titles at the three other Grand Slam tournaments. Following on from the victory by his fellow countryman in the gentlemen's singles final, it was a fitting way to close The Championships. What a fortnight it had been.

Novak Djokovic lifts the Challenge Cup for the second time in his career (opposite)

Nenad Zimonjic and Samantha Stosur pose with their Mixed Doubles trophies

"A VERY SPECIAL FINAL"

"I was just overwhelmed with the emotions, positive emotions, that I was experiencing in the match. I was not surprised, I was just trying to enjoy the moment, rethink what I've been through during the match. Sincerely, this has been the best quality Grand Slam final that I ever been part of."

"Roger played very well, I thought, in a very high level. He showed why he's a champion. He showed a fighting spirit, composure in important moments when he was a break down. When I was serving for the match, he came in and played his best game. I didn't think I did much wrong there."

"It was disappointing losing the fourth set after being so close to win it and match point. But the only way I could have won the match today is by believing that I can make it all the way until the end and staying mentally strong. I didn't allow my emotions to fade away, as it was probably the case in Roland Garros final a couple, three, four weeks ago."

"It was important to start well in the fifth, consolidate my service games, try to put pressure on him. I was the first serving in the fifth set, so he was always behind and trying to catch up. That's something mentally that was in my mind. Just hold your serve and work your way through in the return games and try to wait for the opportunity. When it's presented, you have to grasp it."

"I could have easily lost my concentration in the fifth and just handed him the win.

But I didn't, and that's why this win has a special importance to me mentally. Because I managed to not just win against my opponent but win against myself as well and find that inner strength that got me the trophy today."

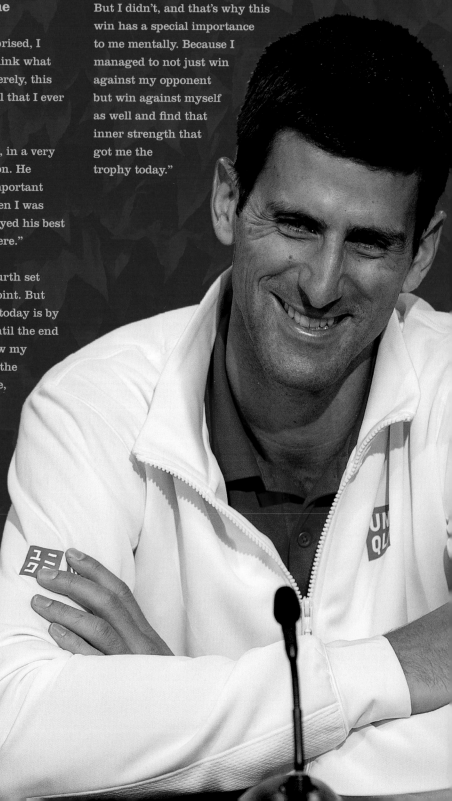

WITH THE DUST SETTLED

The aftermath of the men's singles final at Wimbledon always passes by in a bit of a flurry. Novak Djokovic and Petra Kvitova arrived for the Champions' Dinner at the Royal Opera House with their trophies in hand, before going their separate ways. Djokovic returned to Wimbledon the next day for a media conference, where he was also presented with a gluten-free cake, in recognition of his return to world No.1.

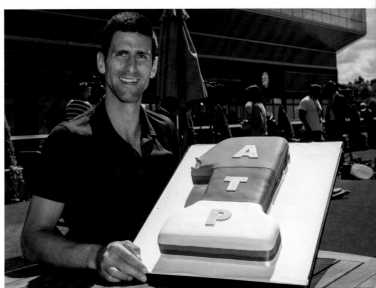

WIMBLEDON 2014

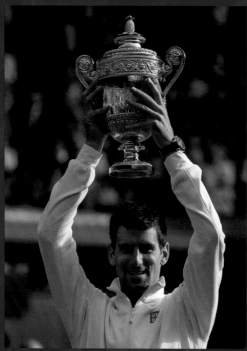

Novak Djokovic
The Gentlemen's Singles

Petra Kvitova
The Ladies' Singles

Jack Sock & Vasek Pospisil
The Gentlemen's Doubles

Roberta Vinci & Sara Errani
The Ladies' Doubles

Nenad Zimonjic & Samantha Stosur
The Mixed Doubles

THE CHAMPIONS

Noah Rubin
The Boys' Singles

Jelena Ostapenko
The Girls' Singles

Orlando Luz & Marcelo Zormann
The Boys' Doubles

Tami Grende & Qiu Yu Ye
The Girls' Doubles

Thomas Enqvist & Mark Philippoussis
The Gentlemen's Invitation Doubles

Guy Forget & Cedric Pioline
The Gentlemen's Senior Invitation Doubles

Jana Novotna & Barbara Schett
The Ladies' Invitation Doubles

Stephane Houdet & Shingo Kunieda
The Gentlemen's Wheelchair Doubles

Jordanne Whiley & Yui Kamiji
The Ladies' Wheelchair Doubles

EVENT I – THE GENTLEMEN'S SINGLES CHAMPIONSHIP 2014

Holder: ANDY MURRAY (GBR)

The Champion will become the holder, for the year only, of the CHALLENGE CUP presented by The All England Lawn Tennis and Croquet Club in 1887. The Champion will receive a silver three-quarter size replica of the Challenge Cup. A Silver Salver will be presented to the Runner up and a Bronze Medal to each defeated semi-finalist. The matches will be the best of five sets.

First Round

1. **Novak Djokovic [1]** *(2)* (SRB)
2. Andrey Golubev *(56)* (KAZ)
3. Radek Stepanek *(38)* (CZE)
4. Pablo Cuevas *(54)* (URU)
5. (Q) Konstantin Kravchuk *(221)* (RUS)
6. Gilles Simon *(44)* (FRA)
7. Robin Haase *(53)* (NED)
8. **Vasek Pospisil [31]** *(33)* (CAN)
9. **Mikhail Youzhny [17]** *(16)* (RUS)
10. (WC) James Ward *(154)* (GBR)
11. (Q) Jimmy Wang *(147)* (TPE)
12. Alejandro Gonzalez *(76)* (COL)
13. Bradley Klahn *(75)* (USA)
14. Sam Querrey *(67)* (USA)
15. Jurgen Melzer *(49)* (AUT)
16. **Jo-Wilfried Tsonga [14]** *(17)* (FRA)
17. **Ernests Gulbis [12]** *(10)* (LAT)
18. Jurgen Zopp *(88)* (EST)
19. Sergiy Stakhovsky *(90)* (UKR)
20. Carlos Berlocq *(43)* (ARG)
21. Jeremy Chardy *(42)* (FRA)
22. (WC) Daniel Cox *(214)* (GBR)
23. Marinko Matosevic *(58)* (AUS)
24. **Fernando Verdasco [18]** *(24)* (ESP)
25. **Marin Cilic [26]** *(29)* (CRO)
26. Paul-Henri Mathieu *(89)* (FRA)
27. Andreas Haider-Maurer *(95)* (AUT)
28. (WC) Kyle Edmund *(320)* (GBR)
29. Bernard Tomic *(86)* (AUS)
30. Evgeny Donskoy *(114)* (RUS)
31. Victor Hanescu *(104)* (ROU)
32. **Tomas Berdych [6]** *(6)* (CZE)
33. **Andy Murray [3]** *(5)* (GBR)
34. David Goffin *(105)* (BEL)
35. Pablo Andujar *(80)* (ESP)
36. Blaz Rola *(92)* (SLO)
37. Tobias Kamke *(87)* (GER)
38. (Q) Jan Hernych *(285)* (CZE)
39. Steve Johnson *(70)* (USA)
40. **Roberto Bautista Agut [27]** *(23)* (ESP)
41. **Kevin Anderson [20]** *(18)* (RSA)
42. (LL) Aljaz Bedene *(140)* (SLO)
43. Filippo Volandri *(117)* (ITA)
44. Edouard Roger-Vasselin *(50)* (FRA)
45. Teymuraz Gabashvili *(61)* (RUS)
46. (Q) Tim Puetz *(251)* (GER)
47. (Q) Alex Kuznetsov *(148)* (USA)
48. **Fabio Fognini [16]** *(15)* (ITA)
49. **Grigor Dimitrov [11]** *(13)* (BUL)
50. (Q) Ryan Harrison *(150)* (USA)
51. (Q) Luke Saville *(236)* (AUS)
52. Dominic Thiem *(57)* (AUT)
53. Donald Young *(69)* (USA)
54. Benjamin Becker *(65)* (GER)
55. (Q) Samuel Groth *(124)* (AUS)
56. **Alexandr Dolgopolov [21]** *(19)* (UKR)
57. **Andreas Seppi [25]** *(36)* (ITA)
58. Leonardo Mayer *(64)* (ARG)
59. Dustin Brown *(79)* (GER)
60. (WC) Marcos Baghdatis *(119)* (CYP)
61. Andrey Kuznetsov *(118)* (RUS)
62. (WC) Daniel Evans *(143)* (GBR)
63. Pablo Carreno Busta *(60)* (ESP)
64. **David Ferrer [7]** *(7)* (ESP)
65. **Stan Wawrinka [5]** *(3)* (SUI)
66. Joao Sousa *(41)* (POR)
67. Yen-Hsun Lu *(47)* (TPE)
68. Aleksandr Nedovyesov *(102)* (KAZ)
69. Michael Russell *(94)* (USA)
70. Julian Reister *(110)* (GER)
71. Denis Istomin *(45)* (UZB)
72. **Dmitry Tursunov [32]** *(31)* (RUS)
73. **Feliciano Lopez [19]** *(26)* (ESP)
74. (Q) Yuichi Sugita *(145)* (JPN)
75. Alejandro Falla *(55)* (COL)
76. (Q) Ante Pavic *(163)* (CRO)
77. Jarkko Nieminen *(62)* (FIN)
78. Federico Delbonis *(37)* (ARG)
79. (WC) Daniel Smethurst *(234)* (GBR)
80. **John Isner [9]** *(11)* (USA)
81. **Jerzy Janowicz [15]** *(25)* (POL)
82. Somdev Devvarman *(125)* (IND)
83. Lleyton Hewitt *(48)* (AUS)
84. Michal Przysiezny *(120)* (POL)
85. Pere Riba *(82)* (ESP)
86. Adrian Mannarino *(81)* (FRA)
87. Lukas Lacko *(88)* (SVK)
88. **Tommy Robredo [23]** *(22)* (ESP)
89. **Marcel Granollers [30]** *(30)* (ESP)
90. Nicolas Mahut *(54)* (FRA)
91. Daniel Gimeno-Traver *(96)* (ESP)
92. Santiago Giraldo *(35)* (COL)
93. (Q) Gilles Muller *(103)* (LUX)
94. Julien Benneteau *(46)* (FRA)
95. Paolo Lorenzi *(83)* (ITA)
96. **Roger Federer [4]** *(4)* (SUI)
97. **Milos Raonic [8]** *(9)* (CAN)
98. Matthew Ebden *(85)* (AUS)
99. (Q) Pierre-Hugues Herbert *(130)* (FRA)
100. Jack Sock *(77)* (USA)
101. Lukasz Kubot *(72)* (POL)
102. Jan-Lennard Struff *(66)* (GER)
103. Dusan Lajovic *(84)* (SRB)
104. **Guillermo Garcia-Lopez [28]** *(34)* (ESP)
105. **Philipp Kohlschreiber [22]** *(28)* (GER)
106. Igor Sijsling *(59)* (NED)
107. (Q) Tatsuma Ito *(129)* (JPN)
108. (LL) Simone Bolelli *(132)* (ITA)
109. (Q) Marsel Ilhan *(151)* (TUR)
110. (Q) Denis Kudla *(136)* (USA)
111. Kenny De Schepper *(73)* (FRA)
112. **Kei Nishikori [10]** *(12)* (JPN)
113. **Richard Gasquet [13]** *(14)* (FRA)
114. (Q) James Duckworth *(161)* (AUS)
115. (WC) Nick Kyrgios *(144)* (AUS)
116. Stephane Robert *(78)* (FRA)
117. (WC) Jiri Vesely *(68)* (CZE)
118. Victor Estrella *(91)* (DOM)
119. (LL) Malek Jaziri *(121)* (TUN)
120. **Gael Monfils [24]** *(21)* (FRA)
121. **Ivo Karlovic [29]** *(32)* (CRO)
122. (LL) Frank Dancevic *(107)* (CAN)
123. Dudi Sela *(101)* (ISR)
124. Mikhail Kukushkin *(63)* (KAZ)
125. Benoit Paire *(71)* (FRA)
126. Lukas Rosol *(52)* (CZE)
127. Martin Klizan *(51)* (SVK)
128. **Rafael Nadal [2]** *(1)* (ESP)

Second Round

- **Novak Djokovic [1]** 6/0 6/1 6/4
- Radek Stepanek 6/2 6/4 6/4
- Gilles Simon 6/2 7/6(4) 7/5
- Robin Haase 7/6(6) 4/6 7/5 6/3
- **Mikhail Youzhny [17]** 6/2 6/2 6/1
- Jimmy Wang 6/3 6/3 6/2
- Sam Querrey 6/7(5) 6/4 6/1 7/5
- **Jo-Wilfried Tsonga [14]** 6/1 3/6 3/6 6/2 6/4
- **Ernests Gulbis [12]** 7/6(7) 7/5 7/6(10)
- Sergiy Stakhovsky 6/3 6/3 6/3
- Jeremy Chardy 6/2 7/6(3) 6/7(6) 6/3
- Marinko Matosevic 6/4 4/6 6/4 6/2
- **Marin Cilic [26]** 6/4 6/7(2) 6/2 6/1
- Andreas Haider-Maurer 6/3 7/6(4) 6/2
- Bernard Tomic 6/4 6/3 6/2
- **Tomas Berdych [6]** 6/7(5) 6/1 6/4 6/3
- **Andy Murray [3]** 6/1 6/4 7/5
- Blaz Rola 6/3 6/1 6/4
- Jan Hernych 6/3 6/7(5) 6/3 5/7 6/4
- **Roberto Bautista Agut [27]** 6/3 6/7(3) 6/4 7/5
- **Kevin Anderson [20]** 6/3 7/5 6/2
- Edouard Roger-Vasselin 7/6(1) 6/2 6/4
- Tim Puetz 2/6 6/4 6/2 6/2
- **Fabio Fognini [16]** 2/6 1/6 6/4 6/1 9/7
- **Grigor Dimitrov [11]** 7/6(1) 6/3 6/2
- Luke Saville 7/5 6/4 3/6 6/4
- Benjamin Becker 6/4 6/3 6/4
- **Alexandr Dolgopolov [21]** 7/5 7/6(2) 7/6(5)
- Leonardo Mayer 6/3 2/6 4/6 7/6(5) 6/4
- Marcos Baghdatis 6/4 7/5 2/6 7/6(4)
- Andrey Kuznetsov 6/1 7/5 3/6 7/6(5)
- **David Ferrer [7]** 6/0 6/7(3) 6/1 6/1
- **Stan Wawrinka [5]** 6/3 6/4 6/3
- Yen-Hsun Lu 6/4 4/6 6/4 1/6 6/1
- Julian Reister 6/4 6/4 6/7(5) 4/6 7/5
- Denis Istomin 7/5 6/4 3/6 6/2
- **Feliciano Lopez [19]** 7/6(6) 7/6(6) 7/6(7)
- Ante Pavic 6/4 6/3 7/5
- Jarkko Nieminen 6/3 7/6(3) 7/5
- **John Isner [9]** 7/5 6/3 6/4
- **Jerzy Janowicz [15]** 4/6 6/3 6/3 3/6 6/3
- Lleyton Hewitt 6/2 6/7(14) 6/1 6/4
- Adrian Mannarino 6/2 6/3 6/4
- **Tommy Robredo [23]** 7/6(5) 1/6 6/2 6/4
- **Marcel Granollers [30]** 6/4 7/6(6) 6/7(7) 6/4
- Santiago Giraldo 6/1 7/5 6/0
- Gilles Muller 6/4 7/6(6) 7/6(5)
- **Roger Federer [4]** 6/1 6/1 6/3
- **Milos Raonic [8]** 6/2 6/4 6/4
- Jack Sock 6/7(5) 6/2 7/6(6) 6/4 6/4
- Lukasz Kubot 7/6(6) 6/4 6/4
- Dusan Lajovic 7/6(5) 6/2 3/6 3/6 6/3
- **Philipp Kohlschreiber [22]** 6/4 6/4 6/2
- Simone Bolelli 7/5 7/6(3) 3/6 7/6(5)
- Denis Kudla 7/6(3) 6/4 4/6 7/5
- **Kei Nishikori [10]** 6/4 7/6(5) 7/5
- **Richard Gasquet [13]** 6/7(3) 6/3 3/6 6/0 6/1
- Nick Kyrgios 7/6(2) 7/6(1) 6/7(6) 6/2
- Jiri Vesely 5/1 Ret'd
- **Gael Monfils [24]** 7/6(5) 7/5 6/4
- Frank Dancevic 6/4 7/6(5) 7/6(4)
- Mikhail Kukushkin 6/4 6/4 6/4
- Lukas Rosol 6/3 3/6 7/6(5) 6/4
- **Rafael Nadal [2]** 4/6 6/3 6/3 6/3

Third Round

- Novak Djokovic [1] 6/4 6/3 6/7(5) 7/6(5)
- Gilles Simon 7/6(1) 6/4 6/4
- Jimmy Wang 7/6(1) 6/2 6/7(5) 6/3
- Jo-Wilfried Tsonga [14] 4/6 7/6(2) 6/7(4) 6/3 14/12
- Sergiy Stakhovsky 6/4 6/3 7/6(5)
- Jeremy Chardy 6/7(5) 7/6(7) 7/6(9) 4/6 7/5
- Marin Cilic [26] 3/6 6/1 6/4 6/4
- Tomas Berdych [6] 4/6 7/6(5) 7/6(3) 6/1
- Andy Murray [3] 6/1 6/1 6/0
- Roberto Bautista Agut [27] 7/5 4/6 6/2 6/2
- Kevin Anderson [20] 7/6(0) 1/6 6/3 6/4
- Fabio Fognini [16] 2/6 6/4 7/6(6) 6/3
- Grigor Dimitrov [11] 6/3 6/2 6/4
- Alexandr Dolgopolov [21] 6/7(4) 7/6(0) 6/3 6/4
- Leonardo Mayer 7/6(4) 4/6 6/1 6/4
- Andrey Kuznetsov 6/7(5) 6/0 3/6 6/3 6/2
- Stan Wawrinka [5] 7/6(6) 6/3 3/6 7/5
- Denis Istomin 7/6(7) 6/4 6/4
- Feliciano Lopez [19] 6/4 7/6(4) 7/5
- John Isner [9] 7/6(17) 7/6(3) 7/5
- Jerzy Janowicz [15] 7/5 6/4 6/7(7) 4/6 6/3
- Tommy Robredo [23] 6/4 6/1 7/6(5)
- Santiago Giraldo 4/6 7/6(2) 1/6 6/1 7/5
- Roger Federer [4] 6/3 7/5 6/3
- Milos Raonic [8] 6/3 6/4 6/4
- Lukasz Kubot 6/7(4) 7/6(4) 6/3 7/6(3)
- Simone Bolelli 4/6 6/4 6/3 2/6 7/5
- Kei Nishikori [10] 6/3 6/2 6/1
- Nick Kyrgios 3/6 6/7(4) 6/4 7/5 10/8
- Jiri Vesely 7/6(3) 6/3 6/7(1) 6/7(3) 6/4
- Mikhail Kukushkin 6/3 6/3 6/2
- Rafael Nadal [2] 4/6 7/6(6) 6/4 6/4

Fourth Round

- Novak Djokovic [1] 6/4 6/2 6/4
- Jo-Wilfried Tsonga [14] 6/2 6/2 7/5
- Jeremy Chardy 6/3 6/7(4) 6/3 6/0
- Marin Cilic [26] 7/6(5) 6/4 7/6(6)
- Andy Murray [3] 6/2 6/3 6/2
- Kevin Anderson [20] 4/6 6/4 2/6 6/2 6/1
- Grigor Dimitrov [11] 6/7(3) 6/4 2/6 6/4 6/1
- Leonardo Mayer 6/4 7/6(1) 6/3
- Stan Wawrinka [5] 6/3 6/3 6/4
- Feliciano Lopez [19] 6/7(8) 7/6(6) 7/6(3) 7/5
- Tommy Robredo [23] 6/2 6/4 6/7(5) 4/6 6/3
- Roger Federer [4] 6/3 6/1 6/3
- Milos Raonic [8] 7/6(2) 7/6(4) 6/2
- Kei Nishikori [10] 3/6 6/3 4/6 7/6(4) 6/4
- Nick Kyrgios 6/3 6/3 7/5 6/2
- Rafael Nadal [2] 6/7(4) 6/1 6/1 6/1

Quarter-Finals

- Novak Djokovic [1] 6/3 6/4 7/6(5)
- Marin Cilic [26] 7/6(8) 6/4 6/4
- Andy Murray [3] 6/4 6/3 7/6(5)
- Grigor Dimitrov [11] 6/4 7/6(6) 6/2
- Stan Wawrinka [5] 7/6(5) 7/6(7) 6/3
- Roger Federer [4] 6/1 6/4 6/4
- Milos Raonic [8] 4/6 6/1 7/6(4) 6/3
- Nick Kyrgios 7/6(5) 5/7 7/6(5) 6/3

Semi-Finals

- Novak Djokovic [1] 6/1 3/6 6/7(4) 6/2 6/2
- Grigor Dimitrov [11] 6/1 7/6(4) 6/2
- Roger Federer [4] 3/6 7/6(5) 6/4 6/4
- Milos Raonic [8] 6/7(4) 6/2 6/4 7/6(4)

Final

- Novak Djokovic [1] 6/4 3/6 7/6(2) 7/6(7)
- Roger Federer [4] 6/4 6/4 6/4

Novak Djokovic [1] 6/7(7) 6/4 7/6(4) 5/7 6/4

Heavy type denotes seeded players. The figure in brackets against names denotes the order in which they have been seeded. The figures in italics denotes ATP World Tour Ranking – 23/06/2014
(WC)=Wild card. (Q)=Qualifier. (LL)=Lucky loser.

EVENT II – THE GENTLEMEN'S DOUBLES CHAMPIONSHIP 2014
Holders: BOB BRYAN (USA) & MIKE BRYAN (USA)

The Champions will become the holders, for the year only, of the CHALLENGE CUPS presented by the OXFORD UNIVERSITY LAWN TENNIS CLUB in 1884 and the late SIR HERBERT WILBERFORCE in 1937. The Champions will receive a silver three-quarter size replica of the Challenge Cup. A Silver Salver will be presented to each of the Runners-up, and a Bronze Medal to each defeated semi-finalist. The matches will be the best of five sets.

First Round	Second Round	Third Round	Quarter-Finals	Semi-Finals	Final

1. **Bob Bryan** (USA) & **Mike Bryan** (USA) ....**[1]**
2. Matthew Ebden (AUS) & Samuel Groth (AUS) ....
   - Bob Bryan & Mike Bryan [1] ... 3/6 7/6(2) 6/2 6/2
(WC) 3. Kyle Edmund (GBR) & Sergiy Stakhovsky (UKR) .....
4. Roberto Bautista Agut (ESP) & Igor Sijsling (NED)...
   - Roberto Bautista Agut & Igor Sijsling ... 4/6 6/4 6/4 6/4
   - Bob Bryan & Mike Bryan [1] ... 6/3 6/4 6/2
   - Bob Bryan & Mike Bryan [1] ... 7/5 6/3 7/6(5)
(Q) 5. Andreas Siljestrom (SWE) & Igor Zelenay (SVK) ......
6. Jonathan Marray (GBR) & John-Patrick Smith (AUS)..
   - Jonathan Marray & John-Patrick Smith ... 6/4 7/5 6/4
(Q) 7. Marcelo Demoliner (BRA) & Purav Raja (IND) ....
8. **Juan-Sebastian Cabal** (COL) & **Marcin Matkowski** (POL)..**[15]**
   - Juan-Sebastian Cabal & Marcin Matkowski [15] ... 6/2 6/4 6/4
   - Juan-Sebastian Cabal & Marcin Matkowski [15] ... 4/6 7/6(5) 6/4 6/3
9. **Julian Knowle** (AUT) & **Marcelo Melo** (BRA) ....**[9]**
10. Martin Emmrich (GER) & Christopher Kas (GER) ......
   - Julian Knowle & Marcelo Melo [9] ... 6/4 7/5 6/3
11. Tomasz Bednarek (POL) & Benoit Paire (FRA) ....
12. Aleksandr Nedovyesov (KAZ) & Dmitry Tursunov (RUS)..
   - Aleksandr Nedovyesov & Dmitry Tursunov ... 6/7(4) 7/6(3) 7/6(2) 6/2
   - Julian Knowle & Marcelo Melo [9] ... 6/1 7/6(9) 6/3
   - Julian Knowle & Marcelo Melo [9] ... 6/3 6/7(2) 7/6(5) 6/3
13. Chris Guccione (AUS) & Lleyton Hewitt (AUS)...........
14. Alejandro Falla (COL) & Marinko Matosevic (AUS)..
   - Chris Guccione & Lleyton Hewitt ... 7/6(5) 6/3 6/3
15. Santiago Giraldo (COL) & Alejandro Gonzalez (COL)..
16. **Lukasz Kubot** (POL) & **Robert Lindstedt** (SWE)**[7]**
   - Lukasz Kubot & Robert Lindstedt [7] ... 6/2 6/1 6/4
   - Chris Guccione & Lleyton Hewitt ... 7/5 6/3 6/4
   - Bob Bryan & Mike Bryan [1] ... 3/6 7/6(6) 6/4 6/4
17. **Julien Benneteau** (FRA) & **Edouard Roger-Vasselin** (FRA)..**[4]**
18. Daniele Bracciali (ITA) & Jonathan Erlich (ISR) ....
   - Julien Benneteau & Edouard Roger-Vasselin [4] ... 6/3 6/7(1) 2/6 6/3 6/4
19. Guillermo Garcia-Lopez (ESP) & Philipp Oswald (AUT)...
20. Andre Begemann (GER) & Lukas Rosol (CZE).........
   - Andre Begemann & Lukas Rosol ... 4/6 6/4 6/3 7/5
   - Julien Benneteau & Edouard Roger-Vasselin [4] ... 6/3 6/7(3) 6/4 6/2
   - Julien Benneteau & Edouard Roger-Vasselin [4] ... 6/7(3) 6/2 7/6(4) 6/3
21. Benjamin Becker (GER) & Oliver Marach (AUT)........
22. Jaroslav Levinsky (CZE) & Jiri Vesely (CZE)............
   - Jaroslav Levinsky & Jiri Vesely ... 6/3 6/7(6) 7/6(7)
23. (Q) Ryan Harrison (USA) & Kevin King (USA)..................
24. **Eric Butorac** (USA) & **Raven Klaasen** (RSA) ....**[13]**
   - Eric Butorac & Raven Klaasen [13] ... 6/4 3/6 6/1 6/4
   - Eric Butorac & Raven Klaasen [13] ... 6/3 6/7(5) 7/6(5) 6/4
   - Michael Llodra & Nicolas Mahut [12] ... 6/4 6/4 5/7 6/4
25. **Michael Llodra** (FRA) & **Nicolas Mahut** (FRA)...**[12]**
26. Federico Delbonis (ARG) & Leonardo Mayer (ARG) ...
   - Michael Llodra & Nicolas Mahut [12] ... 6/3 6/3 6/3
(WC) 27. Edward Corrie (GBR) & Daniel Smethurst (GBR).....
28. Johan Brunstrom (SWE) & Frederik Nielsen (DEN)...
   - Johan Brunstrom & Frederik Nielsen ... 6/4 7/6(4) 7/6(2)
   - Michael Llodra & Nicolas Mahut [12] ... 6/3 6/4 6/2
   - Michael Llodra & Nicolas Mahut [12] ... 7/6(2) 7/5 7/5
29. Nicholas Monroe (USA) & Simon Stadler (GER)........
30. Simone Bolelli (ITA) & Fabio Fognini (ITA)...........
   - Simone Bolelli & Fabio Fognini ... 6/2 6/3 6/1
31. Marin Draganja (CRO) & Florin Mergea (ROU) ....
32. **Marcel Granollers** (ESP) & **Marc Lopez** (ESP) .....**[6]**
   - Marcel Granollers & Marc Lopez [6] ... 6/7(4) 6/1 6/2 3/6 6/1
   - Marcel Granollers & Marc Lopez [6] ... 6/2 7/5 2/6 1/6 6/3
33. **Leander Paes** (IND) & **Radek Stepanek** (CZE)...**[5]**
34. Mariusz Fyrstenberg (POL) & Rajeev Ram (USA)......
   - Leander Paes & Radek Stepanek [5] ... 6/2 7/6(4) 3/6 6/4
35. Santiago Gonzalez (MEX) & Scott Lipsky (USA)......
36. Lukas Dlouhy (CZE) & Paul Hanley (AUS)............
   - Santiago Gonzalez & Scott Lipsky ... 7/6(7) 6/0 3/6 7/6(3)
   - Leander Paes & Radek Stepanek [5] ... 3/6 6/1 3/6 6/3 11/9
   - Leander Paes & Radek Stepanek [5] ... 6/4 6/7(5) 6/4 7/5
37. Feliciano Lopez (ESP) & Jurgen Melzer (AUT) ....
(Q) 38. Alex Bolt (AUS) & Andrew Whittington (AUS).........
   - Feliciano Lopez & Jurgen Melzer ... 7/5 3/6 6/3 6/2
39. Henri Kontinen (FIN) & Jarkko Nieminen (FIN).........
40. **Jean-Julien Rojer** (NED) & **Horia Tecau** (ROU)....**[11]**
   - Jean-Julien Rojer & Horia Tecau [11] ... 7/6(5) 6/4 7/6(4)
   - Jean-Julien Rojer & Horia Tecau [11] ... 7/6(3) 6/3 7/6(8)
41. **Pablo Cuevas** (URU) & **David Marrero** (ESP) ....**[16]**
(WC) 42. Colin Fleming (GBR) & Ross Hutchins (GBR)...........
   - Pablo Cuevas & David Marrero [16] ... 6/3 4/6 6/3 7/6(2)
43. Bradley Klahn (USA) & Michael Venus (NZL)...........
44. Austin Krajicek (USA) & Donald Young (USA)........
   - Austin Krajicek & Donald Young ... 7/5 7/6(5) 4/6 6/0
   - Pablo Cuevas & David Marrero [16] ... 6/4 6/7(4) 7/5 7/5
   - Daniel Nestor & Nenad Zimonjic [3] ... 7/6(8) 6/4 6/4
45. Ken Skupski (GBR) & Neal Skupski (GBR).................
46. Dustin Brown (GER) & Jan-Lennard Struff (GER).....
   - Dustin Brown & Jan-Lennard Struff ... 5/7 6/3 6/4 6/2
47. Paolo Lorenzi (ITA) & Andreas Seppi (ITA).................
48. **Daniel Nestor** (CAN) & **Nenad Zimonjic** (SRB)...**[3]**
   - Daniel Nestor & Nenad Zimonjic [3] ... 7/6(5) 6/3 6/4
   - Daniel Nestor & Nenad Zimonjic [3] ... 6/4 3/6 6/4 6/2
49. **Rohan Bopanna** (IND) & **Aisam Qureshi** (PAK)...**[8]**
50. Frantisek Cermak (CZE) & Mikhail Elgin (RUS)..........
   - Rohan Bopanna & Aisam Qureshi [8] ... 7/6(9) 7/6(8) 6/3
51. Vasek Pospisil (CAN) & Jack Sock (USA)...............
52. Robin Haase (NED) & Jesse Huta Galung (NED)......
   - Vasek Pospisil & Jack Sock ... 6/3 6/2 6/2
   - Vasek Pospisil & Jack Sock ... 6/7(3) 7/6(5) 6/3 4/6 7/6
   - Vasek Pospisil & Jack Sock ... 7/6(3) 7/6(3) 6/4
53. Andrey Golubev (KAZ) & Denis Istomin (UZB)...........
54. Teymuraz Gabashvili (RUS) & Mikhail Kukushkin (KAZ)..
   - Teymuraz Gabashvili & Mikhail Kukushkin ... 7/6(6) 6/4 4/6 7/6(6)
55. Mate Pavic (CRO) & Andre Sa (BRA)...................
56. **Treat Huey** (PHI) & **Dominic Inglot** (GBR)...........**[10]**
   - Mate Pavic & Andre Sa ... 6/4 7/6(5) 6/3
   - Mate Pavic & Andre Sa ... 3/6 7/6(6) 6/4 6/4
57. **Jamie Murray** (GBR) & **John Peers** (AUS)...........**[14]**
(WC) 58. Daniel Evans (GBR) & James Ward (GBR)..............
   - Jamie Murray & John Peers [14] ... 6/2 6/4 6/4
59. Yen-Hsun Lu (TPE) & Divij Sharan (IND) ....
(WC) 60. Jamie Delgado (GBR) & Gilles Muller (LUX)............
   - Jamie Delgado & Gilles Muller ... 2/6 2/6 7/6(3) 6/3 6/2
   - Jamie Murray & John Peers [14] ... 6/3 7/6(7) 6/3
   - Alexander Peya & Bruno Soares [2] ... 6/3 6/7(2) 7/6(3) 3/6 6/3
61. Martin Klizan (SVK) & Dominic Thiem (AUT) ....
62. Carlos Berlocq (ARG) & Joao Sousa (POR)..............
   - Martin Klizan & Dominic Thiem ... 7/5 5/7 6/4 5/7 8/6
63. Max Mirnyi (BLR) & Mikhail Youzhny (RUS)............
64. **Alexander Peya** (AUT) & **Bruno Soares** (BRA)....**[2]**
   - Alexander Peya & Bruno Soares [2] ... 4/6 3/6 6/3 6/2
   - Alexander Peya & Bruno Soares [2] ... 7/6(5) 6/4 6/2

Quarter-Finals / Semi-Finals / Final:

- Bob Bryan & Mike Bryan [1] ... 7/6(4) 6/3 6/2
- Julian Knowle & Marcelo Melo [9] (vs) ...
- Julien Benneteau & Edouard Roger-Vasselin [4] ...
- Michael Llodra & Nicolas Mahut [12] ... 6/4 3/6 7/6(6) 6/4
- Leander Paes & Radek Stepanek [5] ...
- Daniel Nestor & Nenad Zimonjic [3] ...
- Vasek Pospisil & Jack Sock ... 7/6(5) 6/3 6/4
- Alexander Peya & Bruno Soares [2] ...

- Bob Bryan & Mike Bryan [1] ... 3/6 7/6(6) 6/4 6/4
- Michael Llodra & Nicolas Mahut [12]
- Leander Paes & Radek Stepanek [5] ... 3/6 7/6(5) 6/3 6/4
- Vasek Pospisil & Jack Sock

- Bob Bryan & Mike Bryan [1] ... 7/6(4) 6/3 6/2
- Vasek Pospisil & Jack Sock ... 7/6(5) 6/7(3) 6/4 3/6 7/5

Champions: Vasek Pospisil & Jack Sock ... 7/6(5) 6/7(3) 6/4 3/6 7/5

Heavy type denotes seeded players. The figure in brackets against names denotes the order in which they have been seeded.
(WC)=Wild card. (Q)=Qualifier. (LL)=Lucky loser.

EVENT III – THE LADIES' SINGLES CHAMPIONSHIP 2014
Holder: MARION BARTOLI (FRA)

The Champion will become the holder, for the year only, of the CHALLENGE TROPHY presented by The All England Lawn Tennis and Croquet Club in 1886. The Champion will receive a silver three-quarter size replica of the Challenge Trophy. A Silver Salver will be presented to the Runner up and a Bronze Medal to each defeated semi-finalist. The matches will be the best of three sets.

First Round

	Player	Ranking	Nat
	1. **Serena Williams [1]** (1)		(USA)
	2. Anna Tatishvili (113)		(USA)
	3. Chanelle Scheepers (94)		(RSA)
	4. Christina McHale (48)		(USA)
	5. Jovana Jaksic (123)		(SRB)
	6. Petra Cetkovska (62)		(CZE)
	7. Anna Karolina Schmiedlova (58)		(SVK)
	8. **Alize Cornet [25]** (24)		(FRA)
	9. **Andrea Petkovic [20]** (20)		(GER)
	10. Katarzyna Piter (101)		(POL)
	11. Irina-Camelia Begu (81)		(ROU)
	12. Virginie Razzano (97)		(FRA)
(WC)	13. Silvia Soler-Espinosa (75)		(ESP)
	14. Olga Govortsova (105)		(BLR)
	15. Daniela Hantuchova (34)		(SVK)
	16. **Eugenie Bouchard [13]** (13)		(CAN)
	17. **Angelique Kerber [9]** (7)		(GER)
	18. Urszula Radwanska (103)		(POL)
	19. Heather Watson (60)		(GBR)
	20. Ajla Tomljanovic (53)		(CRO)
	21. Petra Martic (127)		(CRO)
	22. Lourdes Dominguez Lino (131)		(ESP)
(Q)	23. Tamira Paszek (121)		(AUT)
	24. **Kirsten Flipkens [24]** (26)		(BEL)
	25. **Anastasia Pavlyuchenkova [26]** (25)		(RUS)
	26. Alison Riske (44)		(USA)
	27. Alexandra Cadantu (83)		(ROU)
	28. Camila Giorgi (39)		(ITA)
(Q)	29. Timea Bacsinszky (85)		(SUI)
	30. Sharon Fichman (84)		(CAN)
(WC)	31. Samantha Murray (247)		(GBR)
	32. **Maria Sharapova [5]** (5)		(RUS)
	33. **Simona Halep [3]** (3)		(ROU)
	34. Teliana Pereira (88)		(BRA)
	35. Dinah Pfizenmaier (116)		(GER)
(Q)	36. Lesia Tsurenko (170)		(UKR)
	37. Belinda Bencic		(SUI)
	38. Magdalena Rybarikova (37)		(SVK)
(Q)	39. Victoria Duval (114)		(USA)
	40. **Sorana Cirstea [29]** (29)		(ROU)
	41. **Roberta Vinci [21]** (21)		(ITA)
	42. Donna Vekic (87)		(CRO)
(WC)	43. Vera Zvonareva (566)		(RUS)
(WC)	44. Tara Moore (250)		(GBR)
	45. Zarina Diyas (72)		(KAZ)
	46. Kristina Mladenovic (107)		(FRA)
	47. Shuai Zhang (33)		(CHN)
	48. **Carla Suarez Navarro [15]** (15)		(ESP)
	49. **Ana Ivanovic [11]** (11)		(SRB)
	50. Francesca Schiavone (76)		(ITA)
	51. Annika Beck (54)		(GER)
	52. Jie Zheng (66)		(CHN)
	53. Karolina Pliskova (50)		(CZE)
	54. Karin Knapp (47)		(ITA)
	55. Julia Glushko (79)		(ISR)
	56. **Sabine Lisicki [19]** (19)		(GER)
	57. **Klara Koukalova [31]** (32)		(CZE)
(WC)	58. Taylor Townsend (147)		(USA)
	59. Madison Keys (30)		(USA)
	60. Monica Puig (52)		(PUR)
(WC)	61. Kristyna Pliskova (98)		(CZE)
	62. Yaroslava Shvedova (65)		(KAZ)
	63. Kaia Kanepi (42)		(EST)
	64. **Jelena Jankovic [7]** (8)		(SRB)
	65. **Victoria Azarenka [8]** (9)		(BLR)
	66. Mirjana Lucic-Baroni (108)		(CRO)
	67. Johanna Larsson (80)		(SWE)
	68. Bojana Jovanovski (45)		(SRB)
(Q)	69. Tereza Smitkova (175)		(CZE)
	70. Su-Wei Hsieh (126)		(TPE)
	71. Coco Vandeweghe (51)		(USA)
	72. **Garbine Muguruza [27]** (28)		(ESP)
	73. **Lucie Safarova [23]** (23)		(CZE)
	74. Julia Goerges (99)		(GER)
	75. Polona Hercog (63)		(SLO)
	76. Paula Ormaechea (90)		(ARG)
	77. Monica Niculescu (67)		(ROU)
	78. Alison Van Uytvanck (89)		(BEL)
(Q)	79. Aleksandra Wozniak (117)		(CAN)
	80. **Dominika Cibulkova [10]** (10)		(SVK)
	81. **Sara Errani [14]** (14)		(ITA)
	82. Caroline Garcia (46)		(FRA)
	83. Tsvetana Pironkova (40)		(BUL)
	84. Varvara Lepchenko (57)		(USA)
	85. Misaki Doi (95)		(JPN)
	86. Elina Svitolina (35)		(UKR)
	87. Kimiko Date-Krumm (70)		(JPN)
	88. **Ekaterina Makarova [22]** (22)		(RUS)
	89. **Svetlana Kuznetsova [28]** (27)		(RUS)
(Q)	90. Michelle Larcher De Brito (102)		(POR)
	91. Stefanie Voegele (77)		(SUI)
(Q)	92. Jarmila Gajdosova (177)		(AUS)
(Q)	93. Anett Kontaveit (176)		(EST)
	94. Casey Dellacqua (36)		(AUS)
(Q)	95. Andreea Mitu (213)		(ROU)
	96. **Agnieszka Radwanska [4]** (4)		(POL)
	97. **Petra Kvitova [6]** (6)		(CZE)
	98. Andrea Hlavackova (118)		(CZE)
	99. Mona Barthel (59)		(GER)
	100. Romina Oprandi (184)		(SUI)
	101. Kurumi Nara (41)		(JPN)
	102. Anna-Lena Friedsam (110)		(GER)
	103. Maria-Teresa Torro-Flor (56)		(ESP)
	104. **Venus Williams [30]** (31)		(USA)
	105. **Sloane Stephens [18]** (18)		(USA)
	106. Maria Kirilenko (109)		(RUS)
	107. Johanna Konta (96)		(GBR)
	108. Shuai Peng (61)		(CHN)
	109. Lauren Davis (55)		(USA)
	110. Alisa Kleybanova (82)		(RUS)
	111. Jana Cepelova (64)		(SVK)
	112. **Flavia Pennetta [12]** (12)		(ITA)
	113. **Caroline Wozniacki [16]** (16)		(DEN)
	114. Shahar Peer (78)		(ISR)
(WC)	115. Naomi Broady (163)		(GBR)
	116. Timea Babos (92)		(HUN)
(Q)	117. Ana Konjuh (189)		(CRO)
	118. Marina Erakovic (68)		(NZL)
	119. Yanina Wickmayer (69)		(BEL)
	120. **Samantha Stosur [17]** (17)		(AUS)
	121. **Elena Vesnina [32]** (49)		(RUS)
	122. Patricia Mayr-Achleitner (74)		(AUT)
(Q)	123. Alla Kudryavtseva (134)		(RUS)
	124. Barbora Zahlavova Strycova (43)		(CZE)
	125. Vania King (73)		(USA)
	126. Yvonne Meusburger (38)		(AUT)
(Q)	127. Paula Kania (183)		(POL)
	128. **Na Li [2]** (2)		(CHN)

Second Round

- Serena Williams [1] — 6/1 6/2
- Chanelle Scheepers — 6/3 6/3
- Petra Cetkovska — 6/2 4/6 7/5
- Alize Cornet [25] — 4/6 6/4 6/2
- Andrea Petkovic [20] — 6/1 6/4
- Irina-Camelia Begu — 1/6 6/4 7/5
- Silvia Soler-Espinosa — 6/2 6/3
- Eugenie Bouchard [13] — 7/5 7/5
- Angelique Kerber [9] — 6/2 6/4
- Heather Watson — 6/3 6/2
- Lourdes Dominguez Lino — 6/0 6/1
- Kirsten Flipkens [24] — 6/4 6/7(3) 6/2
- Alison Riske — 4/6 7/5 6/1
- Camila Giorgi — 6/1 7/6(5)
- Timea Bacsinszky — 6/1 6/3
- Maria Sharapova [5] — 6/1 6/0
- Simona Halep [3] — 6/2 6/2
- Lesia Tsurenko — 6/3 6/0
- Belinda Bencic — 2/6 6/3 6/3
- Victoria Duval — 6/4 3/6 6/1
- Donna Vekic — 6/4 4/6 6/4
- Vera Zvonareva — 6/4 6/7(3) 9/7
- Zarina Diyas — 7/6(4) 6/4
- Carla Suarez Navarro [15] — 6/1 6/2
- Ana Ivanovic [11] — 7/6(6) 6/4
- Jie Zheng — 6/1 6/3
- Karolina Pliskova — 6/7(4) 6/4 10/8
- Sabine Lisicki [19] — 6/2 6/1
- Klara Koukalova [31] — 7/5 6/4
- Madison Keys
- Yaroslava Shvedova — 3/6 6/4 8/6
- Kaia Kanepi
- Victoria Azarenka [8] — 6/3 7/5
- Bojana Jovanovski — 7/6(2) 6/…
- Tereza Smitkova — 6/3 6/3
- Coco Vandeweghe — 6/3 3/6 7/5
- Lucie Safarova [23] — 7/6(3) 7/6(3)
- Polona Hercog — 6/4 6/4
- Alison Van Uytvanck — 7/5 6/3
- Dominika Cibulkova [10] — 6/1 6/2
- Caroline Garcia — 2/6 7/6(3) 7/6
- Varvara Lepchenko — 6/7(6) 6/2 6/2
- Misaki Doi — 6/4 6/1
- Ekaterina Makarova [22] — 3/6 6/4 7/5
- Michelle Larcher De Brito — 3/6 6/3 6/1
- Jarmila Gajdosova — 6/3 7/6(6)
- Casey Dellacqua — 3/6 7/6(4) 6/3
- Agnieszka Radwanska [4] — 6/2 6/1
- Petra Kvitova [6] — 6/3 6/0
- Mona Barthel — 7/5 6/0
- Kurumi Nara — 6/4 6/4
- Venus Williams [30] — 6/4 4/6 6/2
- Maria Kirilenko — 6/2 7/6(6)
- Shuai Peng — 6/4 3/6 6/2
- Lauren Davis — 6/1 6/2
- Flavia Pennetta [12] — 6/2 6/3
- Caroline Wozniacki [16] — 6/3 6/0
- Naomi Broady — 2/6 7/6(7) 6/0
- Ana Konjuh — 6/3 4/6 6/0
- Yanina Wickmayer — 3/6 6/4
- Elena Vesnina [32] — 6/0 6/4
- Barbora Zahlavova Strycova — 6/2 6/2
- Yvonne Meusburger — 7/5 6/3
- Na Li [2] — 7/5 6/2

Third Round

- Serena Williams [1] — 6/1 6/1
- Alize Cornet [25] — 6/4 5/7 6/3
- Andrea Petkovic [20] — 6/4 3/6 6/1
- Eugenie Bouchard [13] — 7/5 6/1
- Angelique Kerber [9] — 6/2 5/7 6/1
- Kirsten Flipkens [24] — 6/2 6/1
- Alison Riske — 7/5 6/2
- Maria Sharapova [5] — 6/2 6/1
- Simona Halep [3] — 6/3 4/6 6/4
- Belinda Bencic — 6/4 6/1
- Vera Zvonareva — 6/4 6/4
- Zarina Diyas — 7/6(12) 5/7 6/2
- Ana Ivanovic [11] — 6/4 6/0
- Sabine Lisicki [19] — 6/3 7/5
- Madison Keys — 7/5 6/7(3) 6/2
- Yaroslava Shvedova — 6/3 6/7(4) 6/2
- Bojana Jovanovski — 6/3 3/6 7/5
- Tereza Smitkova — 6/3 7/6(4)
- Lucie Safarova [23] — 7/6(7) 7/5
- Dominika Cibulkova [10] — 3/6 6/3 8/6
- Caroline Garcia — 7/5 6/2
- Ekaterina Makarova [22] — 7/5 6/4
- Michelle Larcher De Brito — 6/3 4/6 6/2
- Agnieszka Radwanska [4] — 6/4 6/0
- Petra Kvitova [6] — 6/2 6/0
- Venus Williams [30] — 7/6(4) 6/1
- Shuai Peng — 6/0 6/3
- Lauren Davis — 6/4 7/6(4)
- Caroline Wozniacki [16] — 6/3 6/2
- Ana Konjuh — 3/6 6/2 6/2
- Barbora Zahlavova Strycova — 6/4 6/2
- Na Li [2] — 6/2 6/2

Fourth Round

- Alize Cornet [25] — 1/6 6/3 6/4
- Eugenie Bouchard [13] — 6/3 6/4
- Angelique Kerber [9] — 3/6 6/3 6/2
- Maria Sharapova [5] — 6/3 6/0
- Simona Halep [3] — 6/4 6/1
- Zarina Diyas — 7/6(1) 3/6 6/3
- Sabine Lisicki [19] — 6/4 3/6 6/1
- Yaroslava Shvedova — 7/6(7) 6/6 Ret'd
- Tereza Smitkova — 4/6 7/6(5) 10/8
- Lucie Safarova [23] — 6/4 6/2
- Ekaterina Makarova [22] — 7/5 6/3
- Agnieszka Radwanska [4] — 6/2 6/0
- Petra Kvitova [6] — 5/7 7/6(2) 7/5
- Shuai Peng — 0/6 6/3 6/3
- Caroline Wozniacki [16] — 6/3 6/0
- Barbora Zahlavova Strycova — 7/6(5) 7/6(5)

Quarter-Finals

- Eugenie Bouchard [13] — 7/6(5) 7/5
- Angelique Kerber [9] — 7/6(4) 4/6 6/4
- Simona Halep [3] — 6/3 6/0
- Sabine Lisicki [19] — 6/3 3/6 6/4
- Lucie Safarova [23] — 6/0 6/2
- Ekaterina Makarova [22] — 6/3 6/0
- Petra Kvitova [6] — 6/3 6/2
- Barbora Zahlavova Strycova — 6/2 7/5

(results)
- Eugenie Bouchard [13] — 6/3 6/4
- Simona Halep [3] — 6/4 6/0
- Lucie Safarova [23] — 6/3 6/1
- Petra Kvitova [6] — 6/1 7/5

Semi-Finals

- Eugenie Bouchard [13] — 7/6(5) 6/2
- Petra Kvitova [6] — 7/6(6) 6/1

Final

- **Petra Kvitova [6]** — 6/3 6/0

Heavy type denotes seeded players. The figure in brackets against names denotes the order in which they have been seeded. The figures in italics denote WTA World Tour Ranking – 23/06/2014
(WC)=Wild card. (Q)=Qualifier. (LL)=Lucky loser.

EVENT IV – THE LADIES' DOUBLES CHAMPIONSHIP 2014
Holders: SU-WEI-HSIEH (TPE) & SHUAI PENG (CHN)

The Champions will become the holders, for the year only, of the CHALLENGE CUPS presented by H.R.H. PRINCESS MARINA, DUCHESS OF KENT, the late President of The All England Lawn Tennis and Croquet Club in 1949 and The All England Lawn Tennis and Croquet Club in 2001.
The Champions will receive a silver three-quarter size replica of the Challenge Cup. A Silver Salver will be presented to each of the Runners-up and a Bronze Medal to each defeated semi-finalist. The matches will be the best of three sets.

First Round	Second Round	Third Round	Quarter-Finals	Semi-Finals	Final

1. **Su-Wei Hsieh** (TPE) & **Shuai Peng** (CHN)............**[1]**
2. Darija Jurak (CRO) & Megan Moulton-Levy (USA)............

Su-Wei Hsieh & Shuai Peng [1] — 6/2 7/5

(LL) 3. Yuliya Beygelzimer (UKR) & Klaudia Jans-Ignacik (POL)...
4. Dominika Cibulkova (SVK) & Kirsten Flipkens (BEL)............

Yuliya Beygelzimer & Klaudia Jans-Ignacik — 6/4 6/4

Su-Wei Hsieh & Shuai Peng [1] — 6/3 6/3

5. Belinda Bencic (SUI) & Tsvetana Pironkova (BUL)............
6. Kaia Kanepi (EST) & Anna Tatishvili (USA)............

Belinda Bencic & Tsvetana Pironkova — 6/2 6/4

7. Karolina Pliskova (CZE) & Kristyna Pliskova (CZE)............
8. **Timea Babos** (HUN) & **Kristina Mladenovic** (FRA)..**[14]**

Timea Babos & Kristina Mladenovic [14] — 6/3 6/7(5) 12/10

Timea Babos & Kristina Mladenovic [14] — 6/1 6/3

Timea Babos & Kristina Mladenovic [14] — 4/6 7/6(5) 6/2

9. **Alla Kudryavtseva** (RUS) & **Anastasia Rodionova** (AUS)....**[11]**
10. Yanina Wickmayer (BEL) & Shuai Zhang (CHN)............

Alla Kudryavtseva & Anastasia Rodionova [11] — 6/1 6/3

11. Petra Cetkovska (CZE) & Vania King (USA)............
12. Madison Keys (USA) & Alison Riske (USA)............

Madison Keys & Alison Riske — 7/6(5) 6/2

Alla Kudryavtseva & Anastasia Rodionova [11] — 6/2 6/2

13. Alize Cornet (FRA) & Caroline Garcia (FRA)............
14. Hao-Ching Chan (TPE) & Yung-Jan Chan (TPE)............

Alize Cornet & Caroline Garcia — 6/3 2/6 6/4

(WC) 15. Naomi Broady (GBR) & Eleni Daniilidou (GRE)............
16. **Raquel Kops-Jones** (USA) & **Abigail Spears** (USA)..**[7]**

Raquel Kops-Jones & Abigail Spears [7] — 7/6(3) 7/5

Raquel Kops-Jones & Abigail Spears [7] — 6/7(8) 6/4 6/2

Alla Kudryavtseva & Anastasia Rodionova [11] — 7/5 6/4

Timea Babos & Kristina Mladenovic [14] — 6/3 3/6 6/4

17. **Kveta Peschke** (CZE) & **Katarina Srebotnik** (SLO)....**[3]**
18. Andrea Petkovic (GER) & Magdalena Rybarikova (SVK)..

Andrea Petkovic & Magdalena Rybarikova — 7/5 6/3

19. Francesca Schiavone (ITA) & Silvia Soler-Espinosa (ESP)..
(Q) 20. Jarmila Gajdosova (AUS) & Arina Rodionova (AUS)............

Jarmila Gajdosova & Arina Rodionova — 6/3 3/6 6/3

Andrea Petkovic & Magdalena Rybarikova — 6/2 7/5

21. Sandra Klemenschits (AUT) & Raluca Olaru (ROU)............
22. Klara Koukalova (CZE) & Monica Niculescu (ROU)............

Klara Koukalova & Monica Niculescu — 6/1 6/4

23. Christina McHale (USA) & Ajla Tomljanovic (CRO)............
24. **Garbine Muguruza** (ESP) & **Carla Suarez Navarro** (ESP)..**[16]**

Garbine Muguruza & Carla Suarez Navarro [16] — 7/6(4) 6/3

Garbine Muguruza & Carla Suarez Navarro [16] — 6/2 4/6 6/4

Andrea Petkovic & Magdalena Rybarikova — 6/3 7/6(3)

25. **Julia Goerges** (GER) & **Anna-Lena Groenefeld** (GER)....**[10]**
(Q) 26. Vesna Dolonc (SRB) & Daniela Seguel (CHI)............

Julia Goerges & Anna-Lena Groenefeld [10] — 6/2 6/3

27. Eva Hrdinova (CZE) & Bojana Jovanovski (SRB)............
28. Andreja Klepac (SLO) & Maria-Teresa Torro-Flor (ESP)..

Eva Hrdinova & Bojana Jovanovski — 7/6(3) 6/2

Julia Goerges & Anna-Lena Groenefeld [10] — 6/4 6/2

29. Daniela Hantuchova (SVK) & Mirjana Lucic-Baroni (CRO)..
(WC) 30. Johanna Konta (GBR) & Tara Moore (GBR)............

Daniela Hantuchova & Mirjana Lucic-Baroni — 6/4 6/4

31. Irina-Camelia Begu (ROU) & Karin Knapp (ITA)............
32. **Ekaterina Makarova** (RUS) & **Elena Vesnina** (RUS)..**[5]**

Ekaterina Makarova & Elena Vesnina [5] — 6/7(8) 6/4 6/4

Ekaterina Makarova & Elena Vesnina [5] — w/o

Julia Goerges & Anna-Lena Groenefeld [10] — 6/3 6/3

Andrea Petkovic & Magdalena Rybarikova — 6/1 7/6(6)

33. **Serena Williams** (USA) & **Venus Williams** (USA)..**[8]**
34. Oksana Kalashnikova (GEO) & Olga Savchuk (UKR)............

Serena Williams & Venus Williams [8] — 5/7 6/1 6/4

35. Irina Buryachok (UKR) & Elina Svitolina (UKR)............
36. Kristina Barrois (GER) & Stefanie Voegele (SUI)............

Kristina Barrois & Stefanie Voegele — 6/0 6/3

Kristina Barrois & Stefanie Voegele — 3/0 Ret'd

37. Annika Beck (GER) & Kurumi Nara (JPN)............
38. Vera Dushevina (RUS) & Chanelle Scheepers (RSA)............

Vera Dushevina & Chanelle Scheepers — 6/3 6/2

39. Varvara Lepchenko (USA) & Saisai Zheng (CHN)............
40. **Andrea Hlavackova** (CZE) & **Jie Zheng** (CHN)........**[9]**

Andrea Hlavackova & Jie Zheng [9] — 7/5 7/5

Andrea Hlavackova & Jie Zheng [9] — 6/4 6/1

Andrea Hlavackova & Jie Zheng [9] — 7/5 6/0

41. **Lucie Hradecka** (CZE) & **Michaella Krajicek** (NED)..**[13]**
42. Gabriela Dabrowski (CAN) & Alicja Rosolska (POL)............

Lucie Hradecka & Michaella Krajicek [13] — 5/7 6/4 6/2

(WC) 43. Jocelyn Rae (GBR) & Anna Smith (GBR)............
44. Flavia Pennetta (ITA) & Samantha Stosur (AUS)............

Flavia Pennetta & Samantha Stosur — 3/6 7/5 6/3

Flavia Pennetta & Samantha Stosur — 7/5 6/3

45. Mona Barthel (GER) & Janette Husarova (SVK)............
46. Anastasia Pavlyuchenkova (RUS) & Lucie Safarova (CZE)..

Anastasia Pavlyuchenkova & Lucie Safarova — 6/2 6/2

Anastasia Pavlyuchenkova & Lucie Safarova — 2/6 7/6(7) 6/4

Anastasia Pavlyuchenkova & Lucie Safarova — 6/1 7/6(9)

(WC) 47. Martina Hingis (SUI) & Vera Zvonareva (RUS)............
48. **Cara Black** (ZIM) & **Sania Mirza** (IND)............**[4]**

Cara Black & Sania Mirza [4] — 6/2 6/4

Andrea Hlavackova & Jie Zheng [9] — 6/1 4/6 6/3

49. **Ashleigh Barty** (AUS) & **Casey Dellacqua** (AUS)..**[6]**
50. Eugenie Bouchard (CAN) & Heather Watson (GBR)............

Ashleigh Barty & Casey Dellacqua [6] — 6/4 7/6(3)

51. Sharon Fichman (CAN) & Donna Vekic (CRO)............
52. Kimiko Date-Krumm (JPN) & Barbora Zahlavova Strycova (CZE)..

Kimiko Date-Krumm & Barbora Zahlavova Strycova — 6/1 6/2

Ashleigh Barty & Casey Dellacqua [6] — 6/4 6/2

(Q) 53. Pauline Parmentier (FRA) & Laura Thorpe (FRA)............
54. Zarina Diyas (KAZ) & Patricia Mayr-Achleitner (AUT)..

Zarina Diyas & Patricia Mayr-Achleitner — 6/3 3/6 6/3

55. Marina Erakovic (NZL) & Arantxa Parra-Santonja (ESP)..
56. **Anabel Medina Garrigues** (ESP) & **Yaroslava Shvedova** (KAZ)..**[12]**

Anabel Medina Garrigues & Yaroslava Shvedova [12] — 6/4 3/6 6/2

Anabel Medina Garrigues & Yaroslava Shvedova [12] — 6/0 6/0

Ashleigh Barty & Casey Dellacqua [6] — 7/6(4) 6/0

57. **Liezel Huber** (USA) & **Lisa Raymond** (USA)............**[15]**
58. Yvonne Meusburger (AUT) & Katarzyna Piter (POL)............

Liezel Huber & Lisa Raymond [15] — 6/0 7/5

59. Jana Cepelova (SVK) & Anna Karolina Schmiedlova (SVK)..
60. Shuko Aoyama (JPN) & Renata Voracova (CZE)............

Shuko Aoyama & Renata Voracova — 6/1 7/6(3)

Shuko Aoyama & Renata Voracova — 0/6 7/6(5) 6/4

(Q) 61. Lyudmyla Kichenok (UKR) & Nadiia Kichenok (UKR)............
62. Lauren Davis (USA) & Monica Puig (PUR)............

Lyudmyla Kichenok & Nadiia Kichenok — 6/2 7/6(5)

Sara Errani & Roberta Vinci [2] — 5/7 7/6(10) 6/1

63. Jelena Jankovic (SRB) & Alisa Kleybanova (RUS)............
64. **Sara Errani** (ITA) & **Roberta Vinci** (ITA)............**[2]**

Sara Errani & Roberta Vinci [2] — 6/2 6/2

Sara Errani & Roberta Vinci [2] — 7/5 6/3

Sara Errani & Roberta Vinci [2] — 6/4 2/6 6/0

Sara Errani & Roberta Vinci [2] — 6/3 6/2

Sara Errani & Roberta Vinci [2] — 6/1 6/3

Timea Babos & Kristina Mladenovic [14] — 6/1 6/3

Heavy type denotes seeded players. The figure in brackets against names denotes the order in which they have been seeded.
(WC)=Wild card. (Q)=Qualifier. (LL)=Lucky loser.

EVENT V – THE MIXED DOUBLES CHAMPIONSHIP 2014
Holders: DANIEL NESTOR (CAN) & KRISTINA MLADENOVIC (FRA)

The Champions will become the holders, for the year only, of the CHALLENGE CUPS presented by members of the family of the late Mr. S. H. SMITH in 1949 and The All England Lawn Tennis and Croquet Club in 2001. The Champions will receive a silver three-quarter size replica of the Challenge Cup. A Silver Salver will be presented to each of the Runners-up and a Bronze Medal to each defeated semi-finalist. The matches will be the best of three sets.

First Round	Second Round	Third Round	Quarter-Finals	Semi-Finals	Final

1. **Mike Bryan** (USA) & **Katarina Srebotnik** (SLO)....[1]
2. Bye
Mike Bryan & Katarina Srebotnik [1]

3. Henri Kontinen (FIN) & Alla Kudryavtseva (RUS)
4. Chris Guccione (AUS) & Oksana Kalashnikova (GEO)
Chris Guccione & Oksana Kalashnikova 6/3 6/4
Chris Guccione & Oksana Kalashnikova 2/6 6/4 6/3

5. Tomasz Bednarek (POL) & Vania King (USA)
6. Divij Sharan (IND) & Shuko Aoyama (JPN)
Tomasz Bednarek & Vania King 6/4 6/4

7. Bye
8. **Max Mirnyi** (BLR) & **Hao-Ching Chan** (TPE) ....[14]
Max Mirnyi & Hao-Ching Chan [14]
Max Mirnyi & Hao-Ching Chan [14] ......7/6(5) 6/4
Max Mirnyi & Hao-Ching Chan [14] ......6/2 7/6(4)

9. **Jamie Murray** (GBR) & **Casey Dellacqua** (AUS)..[10]
10. Bye
Jamie Murray & Casey Dellacqua [10]

(A) 11. Jesse Huta Galung (NED) & Andreja Klepac (SLO)
12. Daniele Bracciali (ITA) & Karin Knapp (ITA)
Jesse Huta Galung & Andreja Klepac 6/3 3/6 6/1
Jamie Murray & Casey Dellacqua [10] ......7/6(8) 6/7(5) 6/4

13. Mate Pavic (CRO) & Bojana Jovanovski (SRB)
14. Jurgen Melzer (AUT) & Anabel Medina Garrigues (ESP)
Mate Pavic & Bojana Jovanovski ......7/6(6) 7/6(4)

15. Bye
16. **Horia Tecau** (ROU) & **Sania Mirza** (IND) ....[6]
Horia Tecau & Sania Mirza [6]
Horia Tecau & Sania Mirza [6] 6/3 6/3

Max Mirnyi & Hao-Ching Chan [14] 6/2 3/6 6/3
Jamie Murray & Casey Dellacqua [10] 7/5 6/3

17. **Alexander Peya** (AUT) & **Abigail Spears** (USA)..[3]
18. Bye
Alexander Peya & Abigail Spears [3]

19. Lukas Rosol (CZE) & Klara Koukalova (CZE)
20. Martin Klizan (SVK) & Belinda Bencic (SUI)
Martin Klizan & Belinda Bencic 6/4 6/0
Martin Klizan & Belinda Bencic 6/4 6/2

(WC) 21. James Ward (GBR) & Anna Smith (GBR)
22. Nicholas Monroe (USA) & Shuai Zhang (CHN)
Nicholas Monroe & Shuai Zhang 6/2 7/5

23. Bye
24. **Bruno Soares** (BRA) & **Martina Hingis** (SUI)......[13]
Bruno Soares & Martina Hingis [13]
Bruno Soares & Martina Hingis [13] 6/1 6/1

Bruno Soares & Martina Hingis [13] 6/3 5/7 9/7

25. **John Peers** (AUS) & **Ashleigh Barty** (AUS).........[12]
26. Bye
John Peers & Ashleigh Barty [12]

27. Jaroslav Levinsky (CZE) & Janette Husarova (SVK)
28. Dmitry Tursunov (RUS) & Megan Moulton-Levy (USA)
Jaroslav Levinsky & Janette Husarova 6/4 6/4
John Peers & Ashleigh Barty [12] ......w/o

(A) 29. Michael Venus (NZL) & Alicja Rosolska (POL)
30. Lukas Dlouhy (CZE) & Liezel Huber (USA)
Lukas Dlouhy & Liezel Huber 6/3 6/4

31. Bye
32. **Daniel Nestor** (CAN) & **Kristina Mladenovic** (FRA)..[5]
Daniel Nestor & Kristina Mladenovic [5]
Daniel Nestor & Kristina Mladenovic [5] 7/5 6/2

Daniel Nestor & Kristina Mladenovic [5] ......7/6(4) 6/3

Max Mirnyi & Hao-Ching Chan [14] ......7/6(4) 7/5

Daniel Nestor & Kristina Mladenovic [5] ......6/4 7/6(3)

33. **Rohan Bopanna** (IND) & **Andrea Hlavackova** (CZE)..[7]
34. Bye
Rohan Bopanna & Andrea Hlavackova [7]

35. Scott Lipsky (USA) & Jie Zheng (CHN)
(WC) 36. Colin Fleming (GBR) & Jocelyn Rae (GBR)
Colin Fleming & Jocelyn Rae 6/2 6/0
Rohan Bopanna & Andrea Hlavackova [7] 6/4 7/5

(WC) 37. Ross Hutchins (GBR) & Heather Watson (GBR)
38. Mikhail Elgin (RUS) & Anastasia Rodionova (AUS)
Mikhail Elgin & Anastasia Rodionova 6/1 1/6 9/7

39. Bye
40. **Juan-Sebastian Cabal** (COL) & **Raquel Kops-Jones** (USA)..[11]
Juan-Sebastian Cabal & Raquel Kops-Jones [11]
Mikhail Elgin & Anastasia Rodionova 6/2 7/5

Mikhail Elgin & Anastasia Rodionova 3/6 7/5 6/3

41. **Nenad Zimonjic** (SRB) & **Samantha Stosur** (AUS)..[15]
42. Bye
Nenad Zimonjic & Samantha Stosur [15]

43. Martin Emmrich (GER) & Michaella Krajicek (NED)
44. Santiago Gonzalez (MEX) & Yung-Jan Chan (TPE)
Martin Emmrich & Michaella Krajicek 6/2 3/6 6/2
Nenad Zimonjic & Samantha Stosur [15] 6/1 6/2

45. Eric Butorac (USA) & Timea Babos (HUN)
46. Philipp Oswald (AUT) & Yvonne Meusburger (AUT)
Eric Butorac & Timea Babos 6/0 4/6 6/3

47. Bye
48. **Leander Paes** (IND) & **Cara Black** (ZIM) ....[4]
Leander Paes & Cara Black [4]
Eric Butorac & Timea Babos 1/6 6/2 6/3

Nenad Zimonjic & Samantha Stosur [15] 2/6 6/2 8/6

Nenad Zimonjic & Samantha Stosur [15] 6/3 6/1

(A) 49. Andre Sa (BRA) & Renata Voracova (CZE)
50. Bye
Andre Sa & Renata Voracova

51. Andre Begemann (GER) & Olga Savchuk (UKR)
52. Florin Mergea (ROU) & Elina Svitolina (UKR)
Florin Mergea & Elina Svitolina 6/4 3/6 6/1
Florin Mergea & Elina Svitolina 6/4 6/4

(WC) 53. Neal Skupski (GBR) & Naomi Broady (GBR)
54. Robert Farah (COL) & Darija Jurak (CRO)
Neal Skupski & Naomi Broady ......7/5 7/6(5)

55. Bye
56. **David Marrero** (ESP) & **Arantxa Parra-Santonja** (ESP)..[9]
David Marrero & Arantxa Parra-Santonja [9]
Neal Skupski & Naomi Broady 2/6 6/3 6/4

Neal Skupski & Naomi Broady 4/6 6/3 6/4

57. **Aisam Qureshi** (PAK) & **Vera Dushevina** (RUS)..[16]
58. Bye
Aisam Qureshi & Vera Dushevina [16]

59. Frantisek Cermak (CZE) & Lucie Hradecka (CZE)
60. Oliver Marach (AUT) & Karolina Pliskova (CZE)
Oliver Marach & Karolina Pliskova 6/1 6/2
Aisam Qureshi & Vera Dushevina [16] ......3/6 7/6(1) 6/2

61. Dominic Inglot (GBR) & Johanna Konta (GBR)
62. Raven Klaasen (RSA) & Marina Erakovic (NZL)
Dominic Inglot & Johanna Konta ......7/6(5) 6/4

63. Bye
64. **Bob Bryan** (USA) & **Kveta Peschke** (CZE)...........[2]
Bob Bryan & Kveta Peschke [2]
Bob Bryan & Kveta Peschke [2] ......7/6(6) 6/3

Aisam Qureshi & Vera Dushevina [16] 7/5 6/4

Nenad Zimonjic & Samantha Stosur [15] 7/5 6/2

Nenad Zimonjic & Samantha Stosur [15] 6/4 6/3

Heavy type denotes seeded players. The figure in brackets against names denotes the order in which they have been seeded.
(A)=Alternate. (WC)=Wild card.

EVENT VI – THE BOYS' SINGLES CHAMPIONSHIP 2014
Holder: GIANLUIGI QUINZI (ITA)

The Champion will become the holder, for the year only, of a Cup presented by The All England Lawn Tennis and Croquet Club. The Champion will receive a three-quarter size Cup and the Runner-up will receive a Silver Salver.
The matches will be best of three sets.

First Round		
1.	**Andrey Rublev [1]** *(1)*	(RUS)
2.	Henrik Wiersholm *(50)*	(USA)
(Q) 3.	Matteo Berrettini *(65)*	(ITA)
(Q) 4.	Akira Santillan *(67)*	(AUS)
5.	Juan Jose Rosas *(38)*	(PER)
6.	Harry Bourchier *(36)*	(AUS)
7.	Tim Van Rijthoven *(57)*	(NED)
8.	**Jumpei Yamasaki [15]** *(17)*	(JPN)
9.	**Kamil Majchrzak [12]** *(13)*	(POL)
10.	Joao Menezes *(22)*	(BRA)
(WC) 11.	Jamie Malik *(185)*	(GBR)
(Q) 12.	Noah Rubin *(326)*	(USA)
13.	Bogdan Ionut Apostol *(53)*	(ROU)
14.	Yunseong Chung *(26)*	(KOR)
15.	Martin Blasko *(40)*	(SVK)
16.	**Francis Tiafoe [7]** *(8)*	(USA)
17.	**Jaume Munar [4]** *(4)*	(ESP)
18.	Ku Keon Kang *(56)*	(KOR)
19.	Francisco Bahamonde *(24)*	(ARG)
20.	Bogdan Bobrov *(51)*	(RUS)
(WC) 21.	Julian Cash *(92)*	(GBR)
22.	Taylor Harry Fritz *(46)*	(USA)
23.	Nino Serdarusic *(21)*	(CRO)
24.	**Marcelo Zormann [14]** *(16)*	(BRA)
(WC) 25.	**Duck Hee Lee [10]** *(11)*	(KOR)
26.	Filippo Baldi *(35)*	(ITA)
(Q) 27.	Jordi Arconada *(76)*	(ARG)
28.	David Poljak *(48)*	(CZE)
(WC) 29.	Rhett Purcell *(82)*	(GBR)
30.	Alex Rybakov *(25)*	(USA)
31.	Petros Chrysochos *(20)*	(CYP)
32.	**Quentin Halys [5]** *(5)*	(FRA)
33.	**Johan Sebastien Tatlot [8]** *(9)*	(FRA)
34.	Omar Jasika *(29)*	(AUS)
35.	Nicolas Alvarez *(19)*	(PER)
36.	Alex Molcan *(47)*	(SVK)
(WC) 37.	Joel Cannell *(157)*	(GBR)
38.	Jan Zielinski *(30)*	(POL)
39.	Jan Choinski *(28)*	(GER)
40.	**Michael Mmoh [11]** *(12)*	(USA)
41.	**Matias Zukas [13]** *(14)*	(ARG)
42.	Chan-Yeong Oh *(55)*	(KOR)
(LL) 43.	Pedro Iamachkine *(70)*	(PER)
44.	Dennis Uspensky *(68)*	(USA)
45.	Ryotaro Matsumura *(61)*	(JPN)
46.	Nicolae Frunza *(49)*	(ROU)
(WC) 47.	Joshua Sapwell *(165)*	(GBR)
48.	**Orlando Luz [3]** *(3)*	(BRA)
49.	**Stefan Kozlov [6]** *(6)*	(USA)
50.	Rafael Matos *(71)*	(BRA)
(Q) 51.	Pedro Martinez Portero *(33)*	(ESP)
(Q) 52.	Seong Chan Hong *(31)*	(KOR)
53.	Hubert Hurkacz *(58)*	(POL)
54.	Lucas Miedler *(23)*	(AUT)
55.	Daniel Appelgren *(41)*	(SWE)
56.	**Naoki Nakagawa [9]** *(10)*	(JPN)
57.	**Daniil Medvedev [16]** *(18)*	(RUS)
58.	Petar Conkic *(44)*	(SRB)
59.	Marc Polmans *(39)*	(AUS)
60.	Logan Smith *(54)*	(USA)
(WC) 61.	Alexander Sendegeya *(95)*	(GBR)
(Q) 62.	Simon Friis Soendergaard *(102)*	(DEN)
(Q) 63.	Andrea Pellegrino *(78)*	(ITA)
(WC) 64.	**Hyeon Chung [2]** *(34)*	(KOR)

Second Round

- Andrey Rublev [1] 6/1 4/6 6/4
- Matteo Berrettini 6/4 6/3
- Harry Bourchier ...... 6/2 7/6(3)
- Tim Van Rijthoven 6/1 6/2
- Kamil Majchrzak [12] 6/3 6/4
- Noah Rubin 6/2 6/4
- Yunseong Chung ...... 2/6 7/6(6) 6/2
- Francis Tiafoe [7] 6/4 3/6 6/3
- Jaume Munar [4] 2/6 6/2 7/5
- Francisco Bahamonde 6/4 6/1
- Taylor Harry Fritz 6/4 6/2
- Marcelo Zormann [14] ...... 6/7(9) 6/1 9/7
- Filippo Baldi 6/3 6/4
- Jordi Arconada 6/4 7/5
- Alex Rybakov ...... 7/6(5) 3/6 9/7
- Petros Chrysochos 4/6 6/4 6/2
- Johan Sebastien Tatlot [8] 7/5 4/6 12/10
- Alex Molcan ...... 7/6(7) 6/4
- Jan Zielinski 7/5 6/4
- Michael Mmoh [11] ...... 6/7(2) 6/3 6/1
- Matias Zukas [13] 6/4 3/6 6/1
- Pedro Iamachkine ...... 7/6(4) 6/4
- Nicolae Frunza ...... 2/6 7/6(4) 13/11
- Joshua Sapwell 4/6 6/3 6/0
- Stefan Kozlov [6] 6/4 6/1
- Pedro Martinez Portero 6/4 6/2
- Lucas Miedler 6/1 6/2
- Naoki Nakagawa [9] 7/5 6/2
- Petar Conkic ...... 3/6 7/6(5) 2/1 Ret'd
- Logan Smith 7/5 6/2
- Simon Friis Soendergaard 6/3 6/0
- Hyeon Chung [2] 6/1 6/2

Third Round

- Andrey Rublev [1] 4/6 6/3 14/12
- Tim Van Rijthoven ...... 6/4 7/6(7)
- Noah Rubin 6/3 7/5
- Francis Tiafoe [7] ...... 7/6(4) 6/3
- Francisco Bahamonde 7/5 4/6 6/4
- Taylor Harry Fritz ...... 6/4 7/6(3)
- Filippo Baldi 6/3 6/4
- Alex Rybakov 6/4 6/3
- Johan Sebastien Tatlot [8] 6/4 6/2
- Michael Mmoh [11] 6/3 6/2
- Pedro Iamachkine 2/6 7/5 6/2
- Joshua Sapwell 6/4 6/3
- Stefan Kozlov [6] 6/0 6/2
- Naoki Nakagawa [9] 6/2 7/5
- Logan Smith ...... 7/6(0) 6/3
- Hyeon Chung [2] 6/1 6/1

Quarter-Finals

- Tim Van Rijthoven ...... 7/6(6) 4/6 7/5
- Noah Rubin ...... 7/6(4) 4/6 6/3
- Taylor Harry Fritz ...... 6/7(3) 6/3 6/3
- Filippo Baldi 4/6 6/3 6/1
- Johan Sebastien Tatlot [8] 7/5 6/3
- Joshua Sapwell 6/1 6/3
- Stefan Kozlov [6] ...... 6/3 7/6(2)
- Hyeon Chung [2] 6/2 6/3

Semi-Finals

- Noah Rubin ...... 7/6(6) 7/6(5)
- Taylor Harry Fritz ...... 7/5 6/7(5) 7/5
- Johan Sebastien Tatlot [8] ...... 7/6(5) 6/1
- Stefan Kozlov [6] ...... 6/4 7/6(7)

Final

- Noah Rubin 6/4 6/2
- Stefan Kozlov [6] ...... 6/3 7/6(7)

Champion

- Noah Rubin 6/4 4/6 6/3

Heavy type denotes seeded players. The figure in brackets against names denotes the order in which they have been seeded. The Committee reserves the right to alter the seeding order in the event of withdrawals.
(WC) = Wild card. (Q) = Qualifier. (LL) = Lucky Loser.

EVENT VII – THE BOYS' DOUBLES CHAMPIONSHIP 2014
Holders: THANASI KOKKINAKIS (AUS) & NICK KYRGIOS (AUS)

The Champions will become the holders, for the year only, of a Cup presented by The All England Lawn Tennis and Croquet Club. The Champions will receive a three-quarter size Cup and the Runners-up will receive a Silver Salvers.
The matches will be best of three sets.

First Round

1. **Stefan Kozlov (USA) & Andrey Rublev (RUS)** ...... [1]
2. Yunseong Chung (KOR) & Alex Rybakov (USA)
3. Jan Choinski (GER) & Hubert Hurkacz (POL)
4. Seong Chan Hong (KOR) & Ku Keon Kang (KOR)
5. Filippo Baldi (ITA) & Lucas Miedler (AUT)
6. Duck Hee Lee (KOR) & Simon Friis Soendergaard (DEN)
(WC) 7. Joel Cannell (GBR) & Max Stewart (GBR)
8. **Francisco Bahamonde (ARG) & Matias Zukas (ARG)** [6]
9. **Michael Mmoh (USA) & Francis Tiafoe (USA)** [4]
10. Bogdan Bobrov (RUS) & Dennis Uspensky (USA)
11. Matteo Berrettini (ITA) & Andrea Pellegrino (ITA)
12. Rafael Matos (BRA) & Joao Menezes (BRA)
13. Harry Bourchier (AUS) & Marc Polmans (AUS)
14. Jordi Arconada (ARG) & Petar Conkic (SRB)
(WC) 15. Jamie Malik (GBR) & Rhett Purcell (GBR)
16. **Petros Chrysochos (CYP) & Nino Serdarusic (CRO)** [7]
17. **Pedro Martinez Portero (ESP) & Jaume Munar (ESP)** [5]
18. Lloyd George Muirhead Harris (RSA) & Pedro Iamachkine (PER)
19. Omar Jasika (AUS) & Juan Jose Rosas (PER)
20. Daniel Appelgren (SWE) & David Poljak (CZE)
21. Nicolas Alvarez (PER) & Henrik Wiersholm (USA)
22. Taylor Harry Fritz (USA) & Logan Smith (USA)
(WC) 23. Julian Cash (GBR) & Alexander Sendegeya (GBR)
24. **Orlando Luz (BRA) & Marcelo Zormann (BRA)** [3]
25. **Kamil Majchrzak (POL) & Jan Zielinski (POL)** [8]
26. Daniil Medvedev (RUS) & Akira Santillan (AUS)
(WC) 27. Jay Clarke (GBR) & Marcus Walters (GBR)
28. Naoki Nakagawa (JPN) & Tim Van Rijthoven (NED)
29. Ryotaro Matsumura (JPN) & Jumpei Yamasaki (JPN)
30. Bogdan Ionut Apostol (ROU) & Nicolae Frunza (ROU)
31. Martin Blasko (SVK) & Alex Molcan (SVK)
32. **Quentin Halys (FRA) & Johan Sebastien Tatlot (FRA)** [2]

Second Round

- Stefan Kozlov & Andrey Rublev [1] 7/5 7/5
- Jan Choinski & Hubert Hurkacz 5/7 6/3 6/2
- Filippo Baldi & Lucas Miedler 6/2 6/1
- Francisco Bahamonde & Matias Zukas [6] 6/3 6/4
- Michael Mmoh & Francis Tiafoe [4] 6/4 6/4
- Rafael Matos & Joao Menezes 6/1 6/2
- Harry Bourchier & Marc Polmans 6/4 7/5
- Petros Chrysochos & Nino Serdarusic [7] 6/4 3/6 6/3
- Pedro Martinez Portero & Jaume Munar [5] 6/1 4/6 6/3
- Daniel Appelgren & David Poljak ...... 6/7(5) 7/5 6/4
- Nicolas Alvarez & Henrik Wiersholm ...... 7/6(5) 6/2
- Orlando Luz & Marcelo Zormann [3] ...... 6/2 6/7(5) 6/3
- Daniil Medvedev & Akira Santillan ...... 7/6(3) 6/3
- Naoki Nakagawa & Tim Van Rijthoven 6/1 3/6 6/0
- Ryotaro Matsumura & Jumpei Yamasaki ...... 6/7(5) 6/4 6/3
- Quentin Halys & Johan Sebastien Tatlot [2] ...... w/o

Quarter-Finals

- Stefan Kozlov & Andrey Rublev [1] ...... 7/6(4) 6/2
- Filippo Baldi & Lucas Miedler ...... 6/7(9) 6/3 6/2
- Rafael Matos & Joao Menezes ...... 6/1 7/6(14)
- Petros Chrysochos & Nino Serdarusic [7] 4/1 6/4
- Pedro Martinez Portero & Jaume Munar [5] ...... 6/7(4) 7/6(5) 6/3
- Orlando Luz & Marcelo Zormann [3] 6/2 6/4
- Naoki Nakagawa & Tim Van Rijthoven ...... w/o
- Quentin Halys & Johan Sebastien Tatlot [2] ...... 6/4 7/6(3)

Semi-Finals

- Stefan Kozlov & Andrey Rublev [1] ...... 7/6(5) 6/2
- Petros Chrysochos & Nino Serdarusic [7] ...... 6/2 6/7(1) 9/7
- Orlando Luz & Marcelo Zormann [3] 6/3 6/3
- Naoki Nakagawa & Tim Van Rijthoven ...... 6/3 7/6(7)

Final

- Stefan Kozlov & Andrey Rublev [1] 6/2 7/5
- Orlando Luz & Marcelo Zormann [3] 6/3 5/7 6/4

Champions

- Orlando Luz & Marcelo Zormann [3] 6/4 3/6 8/6

Heavy type denotes seeded players. The figure in brackets against names denotes the order in which they have been seeded. The Committee reserves the right to alter the seeding order in the event of withdrawals.
(WC) = Wild card. (Q) = Qualifier. (LL) = Lucky Loser.

EVENT VIII – THE GIRLS' SINGLES CHAMPIONSHIP 2014

Holder: BELINDA BENCIC (SUI)

The Champion will become the holder, for the year only, of a Cup presented by The All England Lawn Tennis and Croquet Club. The Champion will receive a three-quarter size Cup and the Runner-up will receive a Silver Salver. The matches will be best of three sets.

First Round

1. **Ivana Jorovic [1]** *(7)* (SRB)
2. Kaitlyn McCarthy *(57)* (USA)
3. Paula Badosa Gibert *(22)* (ESP)
4. Luisa Stefani *(42)* (BRA)
5. (WC) Gabriella Taylor *(93)* (GBR)
6. (Q) Katherine Sebov *(99)* (CAN)
7. Tami Grende *(71)* (INA)
8. **Anna Bondar [15]** *(19)* (HUN)
9. **Marketa Vondrousova [12]** *(14)* (CZE)
10. (WC) Freya Christie *(83)* (GBR)
11. Katrine Isabel Steffensen *(51)* (USA)
12. Viktoria Kuzmova *(46)* (SVK)
13. Seone Mendez *(66)* (AUS)
14. (Q) Holly Hutchinson *(306)* (GBR)
15. Jaqueline Adina Cristian *(49)* (ROU)
16. **Francoise Abanda [7]** *(195)* (CAN)
17. **Tornado Alicia Black [3]** *(4)* (USA)
18. (Q) Anna Brogan *(223)* (GBR)
19. Marie Bouzkova *(31)* (CZE)
20. (WC) Rebecca Sramkova *(256)* (SVK)
21. Margot Yerolymos *(94)* (FRA)
22. (Q) Yolimar Ogando *(84)* (PUR)
23. Katie Boulter *(24)* (GBR)
24. **Priscilla Hon [13]** *(16)* (AUS)
25. **Anhelina Kalinina [9]** *(48)* (UKR)
26. (WC) Harriet Dart *(141)* (GBR)
27. Dasha Ivanova *(36)* (USA)
28. Qiu Yu Ye *(60)* (CHN)
29. (WC) Anastasia Mikheeva *(218)* (GBR)
30. Jelena Ostapenko *(41)* (LAT)
31. Natalia Vikhlyantseva *(52)* (RUS)
32. **Iryna Shymanovich [6]** *(7)* (BLR)
33. **Jil Belen Teichmann [5]** *(6)* (SUI)
34. Fanny Stollar *(29)* (HUN)
35. Evgeniya Levashova *(44)* (RUS)
36. Bianca Turati *(45)* (ITA)
37. Raveena Kingsley *(61)* (USA)
38. Simona Heinova *(38)* (CZE)
39. (WC) Emily Arbuthnott *(95)* (GBR)
40. **Shilin Xu [10]** *(12)* (CHN)
41. **Naiktha Bains [16]** *(21)* (AUS)
42. Greetje Minnen *(39)* (BEL)
43. Sofia Kenin *(28)* (USA)
44. Leticia Garcia Vidal *(43)* (BRA)
45. (WC) Jodie Anna Burrage *(209)* (GBR)
46. (Q) Ipek Soylu *(257)* (TUR)
47. Elena Gabriela Ruse *(54)* (ROU)
48. **Aliona Bolsova Zadoinov [4]** *(5)* (ESP)
49. **Kristina Schmiedlova [8]** *(11)* (SVK)
50. Usue Maitane Arconada *(34)* (USA)
51. Helen Ploskina *(50)* (UKR)
52. Kimberly Birrell *(23)* (AUS)
53. Renata Zarazua *(27)* (MEX)
54. (Q) Justina Mikulskyte *(90)* (LTU)
55. Katie Swan *(76)* (GBR)
56. **Ioana Loredana Rosca [11]** *(13)* (ROU)
57. **Sandra Samir [14]** *(18)* (EGY)
58. (Q) Michaela Gordon *(79)* (USA)
59. Isabelle Wallace *(53)* (GBR)
60. Julia Grabher *(63)* (AUT)
61. (Q) Dalma Galfi *(70)* (HUN)
62. Jana Fett *(26)* (CRO)
63. (WC) Maia Lumsden *(85)* (GBR)
64. **Catherine Cartan Bellis [2]** *(2)* (USA)

Second Round

- **Ivana Jorovic [1]** 6/1 4/6 6/3
- Paula Badosa Gibert 6/3 6/0
- Gabriella Taylor 7/5 6/1
- Tami Grende 6/1 6/4
- **Marketa Vondrousova [12]** 7/6(5) 6/2
- Viktoria Kuzmova 6/4 6/4
- Seone Mendez 6/3 2/6 8/6
- **Francoise Abanda [7]** 6/3 6/2
- **Tornado Alicia Black [3]** 6/3 6/4
- Rebecca Sramkova 6/3 6/3
- Margot Yerolymos 6/1 7/6(1)
- Katie Boulter 6/3 6/3
- **Anhelina Kalinina [9]** 2/6 7/6(2) 6/3
- Dasha Ivanova 7/6(4) 4/6 6/2
- Jelena Ostapenko 6/4 6/3
- Natalia Vikhlyantseva 6/1 6/3
- **Jil Belen Teichmann [5]** 6/2 7/5
- Evgeniya Levashova 6/3 0/6 6/3
- Simona Heinova 7/6(1) 6/4
- **Shilin Xu [10]** 6/3 6/2
- Greetje Minnen 6/3 6/4
- Sofia Kenin 6/4 6/2
- Ipek Soylu 6/4 6/3
- Elena Gabriela Ruse 6/4 6/1
- **Kristina Schmiedlova [8]** 6/1 6/2
- Kimberly Birrell 2/6 7/5 6/3
- Justina Mikulskyte 2/6 6/2 9/7
- **Ioana Loredana Rosca [11]** 6/4 6/4
- Michaela Gordon 6/1 3/6 6/0
- Isabelle Wallace 6/1 6/2
- Dalma Galfi 7/5 6/3
- Maia Lumsden 6/7(4) 6/3 6/4

Third Round

- Paula Badosa Gibert 6/2 7/5
- Gabriella Taylor 6/4 6/4
- **Marketa Vondrousova [12]** 6/3 6/2
- **Francoise Abanda [7]** 6/0 6/4
- **Tornado Alicia Black [3]** 6/2 6/4
- Katie Boulter 6/3 6/3
- **Anhelina Kalinina [9]** 6/1 6/2
- Jelena Ostapenko 7/6(7) 4/6 6/2
- **Jil Belen Teichmann [5]** 7/5 4/6 6/4
- **Shilin Xu [10]** 5/0 Ret'd
- Greetje Minnen 3/6 6/2 6/4
- Elena Gabriela Ruse 2/6 6/1 6/4
- **Kristina Schmiedlova [8]** 6/1 7/5
- **Ioana Loredana Rosca [11]** 7/6(5) 1/6 7/5
- Michaela Gordon 6/2 5/7 8/6
- Maia Lumsden 7/5 6/3

Quarter-Finals

- Paula Badosa Gibert 7/6(5) 6/4
- **Marketa Vondrousova [12]** 7/6(6) 6/7(5) 6/2
- **Tornado Alicia Black [3]** 6/1 6/2
- Jelena Ostapenko 6/2 6/2
- **Shilin Xu [10]** 6/7(3) 6/3 6/1
- Elena Gabriela Ruse 6/4 6/2
- **Kristina Schmiedlova [8]** 6/2 6/4
- Michaela Gordon 6/2 6/1

Semi-Finals

- **Marketa Vondrousova [12]** 6/3 6/2
- Jelena Ostapenko 6/3 6/1
- Elena Gabriela Ruse 6/4 6/3
- **Kristina Schmiedlova [8]** 6/3 6/3

Final

- Jelena Ostapenko 6/1 6/2
- **Kristina Schmiedlova [8]** 4/6 6/3 6/4

Winner: Jelena Ostapenko 2/6 6/3 6/0

Heavy type denotes seeded players. The figure in brackets against names denotes the order in which they have been seeded. The Committee reserves the right to alter the seeding order in the event of withdrawals. (WC) = Wild card. (Q) = Qualifier. (LL) = Lucky Loser.

EVENT IX – THE GIRLS' DOUBLES CHAMPIONSHIP 2014

Holders: BARBORA KREJCIKOVA (CZE) & KATERINA SINIAKOVA (CZE)

The Champions will become the holders, for the year only, of a Cup presented by The All England Lawn Tennis and Croquet Club. The Champions will receive a three-quarter size Cup and the Runners-up will receive a Silver Salvers. The matches will be best of three sets.

First Round

1. **Anhelina Kalinina** (UKR) & **Iryna Shymanovich** (BLR) [1]
2. Ipek Soylu (TUR) & Shilin Xu (CHN)
3. Dasha Ivanova (USA) & Katrine Isabel Steffensen (USA)
4. Kimberly Birrell (AUS) & Greetje Minnen (BEL)
5. Jaqueline Adina Cristian (ROU) & Elena Gabriela Ruse (ROU)
6. (WC) Maia Lumsden (GBR) & Gabriella Taylor (GBR)
7. Tami Grende (INA) & Qiu Yu Ye (CHN)
8. **Jana Fett** (CRO) & **Ioana Loredana Rosca** (ROU) [6]
9. **Katie Boulter** (GBR) & **Ivana Jorovic** (SRB) [4]
10. Evgeniya Levashova (RUS) & Seone Mendez (AUS)
11. Helen Ploskina (UKR) & Julia Terziyska (BUL)
12. Luisa Stefani (BRA) & Renata Zarazua (MEX)
13. (WC) Anna Brogan (GBR) & Harriet Dart (GBR)
14. Usue Maitane Arconada (USA) & Fanny Stollar (HUN)
15. Michaela Gordon (USA) & Sofia Kenin (USA)
16. **Viktoria Kuzmova** (SVK) & **Kristina Schmiedlova** (SVK) [8]
17. (A) Emily Appleton (GBR) & Eden Richardson (GBR)
18. (WC) Emily Arbuthnott (GBR) & Holly Hutchinson (GBR)
19. Lucie Wargnier (FRA) & Margot Yerolymos (FRA)
20. Marie Bouzkova (CZE) & Dalma Galfi (HUN)
21. Freya Christie (GBR) & Isabelle Wallace (GBR)
22. (A) Emilie Francati (DEN) & Verena Hofer (ITA)
23. Raveena Kingsley (USA) & Kaitlyn McCarthy (USA)
24. **Naiktha Bains** (AUS) & **Tornado Alicia Black** (USA) [3]
25. **Paula Badosa Gibert** (ESP) & **Aliona Bolsova Zadoinov** (ESP) [5]
26. Katherine Sebov (CAN) & Leticia Garcia Vidal (BRA)
27. Regina Clark (MEX) & Yolimar Ogando (PUR)
28. Justina Mikulskyte (LTU) & Natalia Vikhlyantseva (RUS)
29. (WC) Jodie Anna Burrage (GBR) & Anastasia Mikheeva (GBR)
30. Anna Bondar (HUN) & Jelena Ostapenko (LAT)
31. Julia Grabher (AUT) & Bianca Turati (ITA)
32. **Priscilla Hon** (AUS) & **Jil Belen Teichmann** (SUI) [2]

Second Round

- **Anhelina Kalinina** & **Iryna Shymanovich** [1] 7/6(2) 6/4
- Dasha Ivanova & Katrine Isabel Steffensen 6/3 6/3
- Jaqueline Adina Cristian & Elena Gabriela Ruse 6/4 7/5(5)
- Tami Grende & Qiu Yu Ye 5/7 7/5 6/4
- **Katie Boulter** & **Ivana Jorovic** [4] 6/3 6/1
- Helen Ploskina & Julia Terziyska 3/6 7/6(6) 6/3
- Usue Maitane Arconada & Fanny Stollar 4/6 6/1 6/4
- **Viktoria Kuzmova** & **Kristina Schmiedlova** [8] 4/6 6/2 6/0
- Emily Arbuthnott & Holly Hutchinson 6/3 6/4
- Marie Bouzkova & Dalma Galfi 6/3 7/6(1)
- Freya Christie & Isabelle Wallace w/o
- **Naiktha Bains** & **Tornado Alicia Black** [3] 6/1 1/6 6/1
- Katherine Sebov & Leticia Garcia Vidal 7/5 3/6 6/2
- Justina Mikulskyte & Natalia Vikhlyantseva 6/4 6/7(6) 6/1
- Anna Bondar & Jelena Ostapenko 6/3 6/2
- **Priscilla Hon** & **Jil Belen Teichmann** [2] 6/3 6/4

Quarter-Finals

- **Anhelina Kalinina** & **Iryna Shymanovich** [1] 6/3 4/6 6/1
- Tami Grende & Qiu Yu Ye 6/4 4/6 6/3
- **Katie Boulter** & **Ivana Jorovic** [4] 6/3 6/1
- Usue Maitane Arconada & Fanny Stollar 5/7 6/4 6/3
- Marie Bouzkova & Dalma Galfi 6/3 6/2
- **Naiktha Bains** & **Tornado Alicia Black** [3] 7/6(7) 6/4
- Katherine Sebov & Leticia Garcia Vidal w/o
- **Priscilla Hon** & **Jil Belen Teichmann** [2] 7/5 6/1

Semi-Finals

- Tami Grende & Qiu Yu Ye 7/6(3) 7/5
- Usue Maitane Arconada & Fanny Stollar 7/6(5) 5/7 9/7
- Marie Bouzkova & Dalma Galfi 6/1 2/6 6/3
- **Priscilla Hon** & **Jil Belen Teichmann** [2] 6/3 6/1

Final

- Tami Grende & Qiu Yu Ye 5/7 6/3 6/4
- Marie Bouzkova & Dalma Galfi 6/1 4/6 9/7

Winners: Tami Grende & Qiu Yu Ye 6/2 7/6(5)

Heavy type denotes seeded players. The figure in brackets against names denotes the order in which they have been seeded. The Committee reserves the right to alter the seeding order in the event of withdrawals. (WC) = Wild card. (Q) = Qualifier. (LL) = Lucky Loser.

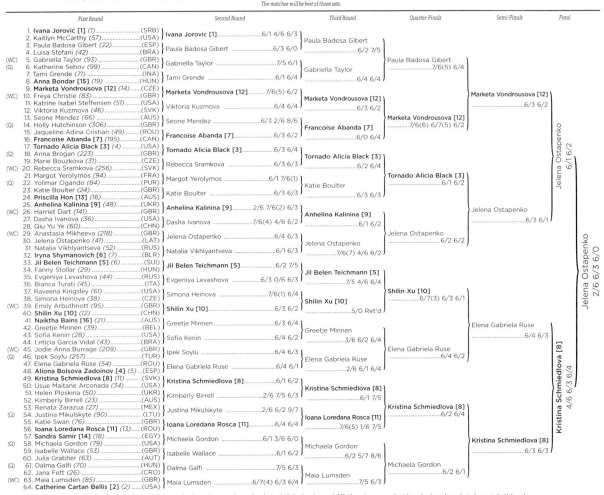

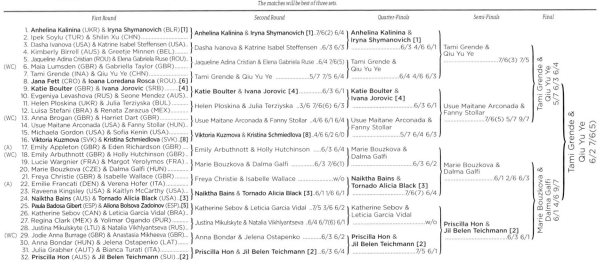

EVENT X – THE GENTLEMEN'S INVITATION DOUBLES 2014
Holders: THOMAS ENQVIST (SWE) & MARK PHILIPPOUSSIS (AUS)

The Champions will become the holders, for the year only, of a Cup presented by The All England Lawn Tennis and Croquet Club. The Champions will receive a silver three-quarter size Cup. A Silver Medal will be presented to each of the Runners-up. The matches will be the best of three sets. If a match should reach one set all a 10 point tie-break will replace the third set.

GROUP A	Jonas Bjorkman (SWE) & Todd Woodbridge (AUS)	Thomas Enqvist (SWE) & Mark Philippoussis (AUS)	Justin Gimelstob (USA) & Chris Wilkinson (GBR)	Goran Ivanisevic (CRO) & Ivan Ljubicic (CRO)	Wins	Losses	Final
Jonas Bjorkman (SWE) & Todd Woodbridge (AUS)		3/6 6/7(5) L	1/1 Ret'd W	6/4 7/6(4) W	2	1	
Thomas Enqvist (SWE) & Mark Philippoussis (AUS)	6/3 7/6(5) W		6/4 3/6 [10-4] W	6/4 6/7(6) [10-5] W	3	0	Thomas Enqvist (SWE) & Mark Philippoussis (AUS)
Justin Gimelstob (USA) & Chris Wilkinson (GBR)	1/1 Ret'd L	4/6 6/3 [4-10] L		6/3 1/6 [7-10] L	0	3	
Goran Ivanisevic (CRO) & Ivan Ljubicic (CRO)	4/6 6/7(4) L	4/6 7/6(6) [5-10] L	3/6 6/1 [10-7] W		1	2	

GROUP B	Albert Costa (ESP) & Thomas Johansson (SWE)	Jacco Eltingh (NED) & Paul Haarhuis (NED)	Wayne Ferreira (RSA) & Mark Petchey (GBR)	Greg Rusedski (GBR) & Fabrice Santoro (FRA)	Wins	Losses	
Albert Costa (ESP) & Thomas Johansson (SWE)		3/6 4/6 L	7/5 5/7 [10-8] W	6/4 6/7(2) [7-10] L	1	2	
Jacco Eltingh (NED) & Paul Haarhuis (NED)	6/3 6/4 W		7/5 7/5 W	6/3 6/4 W	3	0	Jacco Eltingh (NED) & Paul Haarhuis (NED)
Wayne Ferreira (RSA) & Mark Petchey (GBR)	5/7 7/5 [8-10] L	5/7 5/7 L		2/6 5/7 L	0	3	
Greg Rusedski (GBR) & Fabrice Santoro (FRA)	4/6 7/6(2) [10-7] W	3/6 4/6 L	6/2 7/5 W		2	1	

Final: Thomas Enqvist & Mark Philippoussis 3/6 6/3 [10-3]

This event will be played on a 'round robin' basis. Eight invited pairs have been divided into two groups and each pair in each group will play one another. The pairs winning most matches will be the champions of their respective groups and will play each other in the final as indicated above. If matches should be equal in any group, the head-to-head result between the two pairs with the same number of wins will determine the winning pair of the group.

EVENT XI – THE GENTLEMEN'S SENIOR INVITATION DOUBLES 2014
Holders: PAT CASH (AUS) & MARK WOODFORDE (AUS)

The Champions will become the holders, for the year only, of a Cup presented by The All England Lawn Tennis and Croquet Club. The Champions will receive a silver half-size Cup. A Silver Medal will be presented to each of the Runners-up. The matches will be the best of three sets. If a match should reach one set all a 10 point tie-break will replace the third set.

GROUP A	Mansour Bahrami (IRI) & Henri Leconte (FRA)	Peter Fleming (USA) & Patrick McEnroe (USA)	Rick Leach (USA) & Mark Woodforde (AUS)	Peter McNamara (AUS) & Paul McNamee (AUS)	Wins	Losses	Final
Mansour Bahrami (IRI) & Henri Leconte (FRA)		7/6(4) 6/3 W	3/6 6/7(7) L	7/5 6/4 W	2	1	
Peter Fleming (USA) & Patrick McEnroe (USA)	6/7(4) 3/6 L		2/6 4/6 L	6/1 6/4 W	1	2	Rick Leach (USA) & Mark Woodforde (AUS)
Rick Leach (USA) & Mark Woodforde (AUS)	6/3 7/6(7) W	6/2 6/4 W		6/2 7/5 W	3	0	
Peter McNamara (AUS) & Paul McNamee (AUS)	5/7 4/6 L	1/6 4/6 L	2/6 5/7 L		0	3	

GROUP B	Jeremy Bates (GBR) & Anders Jarryd (SWE)	Sergio Casal (ESP) & Joakim Nystrom (SWE)	Andrew Castle (GBR) & Mikael Pernfors (SWE)	Guy Forget (FRA) & Cedric Pioline (FRA)	Wins	Losses	
Jeremy Bates (GBR) & Anders Jarryd (SWE)		6/2 6/4 W	3/6 4/6 L	1/6 7/6(1) [6-10] L	1	2	
Sergio Casal (ESP) & Joakim Nystrom (SWE)	2/6 4/6 L		2/5 Ret'd L	3/6 2/6 L	0	3	Guy Forget (FRA) & Cedric Pioline (FRA)
Andrew Castle (GBR) & Mikael Pernfors (SWE)	6/3 6/4 W	5/2 Ret'd W		3/6 4/6 L	2	1	
Guy Forget (FRA) & Cedric Pioline (FRA)	6/1 6/7(1) [10-6] W	6/3 6/2 W	6/3 6/4 W		3	0	

Final: Guy Forget & Cedric Pioline 6/4 6/3

This event will be played on a 'round robin' basis. Eight invited pairs have been divided into two groups and each pair in each group will play one another. The pairs winning most matches will be the champions of their respective groups and will play each other in the final as indicated above. If matches should be equal in any group, the head-to-head result between the two pairs with the same number of wins will determine the winning pair of the group.

ALPHABETICAL LIST – INVITATION DOUBLES EVENTS
GENTLEMEN

Bjorkman, Jonas (Sweden)
Costa, Albert (Spain)
Eltingh, Jacco (Netherlands)
Enqvist, Thomas (Sweden)
Ferreira, Wayne (South Africa)
Gimelstob, Justin (USA)
Haarhuis, Paul (Netherlands)
Ivanisevic, Goran (Croatia)
Johansson, Thomas (Sweden)
Ljubicic, Ivan (Croatia)
Petchey, Mark (Great Britain)
Philippoussis, Mark (Australia)
Rusedski, Greg (Great Britain)
Santoro, Fabrice (France)
Wilkinson, Chris (Great Britain)
Woodbridge, Todd (Australia)

LADIES

Austin, Tracy (USA)
Davenport, Lindsay (USA)
Fernandez, Mary Joe (USA)
Jaeger, Andrea (USA)
Keothavong, Anne (Great Britain)
Majoli, Iva (Croatia)
Maleeva, Magdalena (Bulgaria)
Martinez, Conchita (Spain)
Navratilova, Martina (USA)
Novotna, Jana (Czech Republic)
Schett, Barbara (Austria)
Sfar, Selima (Tunisia)
Stubbs, Rennae (Australia)
Sukova, Helena (Czech Republic)
Tauziat, Nathalie (France)
Temesvari, Andrea (Hungary)

ALPHABETICAL LIST – GENTLEMEN'S SENIOR INVITATION DOUBLES EVENTS

Bahrami, Mansour (Iran)
Bates, Jeremy (Great Britain)
Casal, Sergio (Spain)
Castle, Andrew (Great Britain)
Fleming, Peter (USA)
Forget, Guy (France)
Jarryd, Anders (Sweden)
Leach, Rick (USA)
Leconte, Henri (France)
McEnroe, Patrick (USA)
McNamara, Peter (Australia)
McNamee, Paul (Australia)
Nystrom, Joakim (Sweden)
Pernfors, Mikael (Sweden)
Pioline, Cedric (France)
Woodforde, Mark (Australia)

EVENT XII – THE LADIES' INVITATION DOUBLES 2014
Holders: LINDSAY DAVENPORT (USA) & MARTINA HINGIS SUI)

The Champions will become the holders, for the year only, of a Cup presented by The All England Lawn Tennis and Croquet Club. The Champions will receive a silver three-quarter size Cup. A Silver Medal will be presented to each of the Runners-up. The matches will be the best of three sets. If a match should reach one set all a 10 point tie-break will replace the third set.

GROUP A	Lindsay Davenport (USA) & Mary Joe Fernandez (USA)	Anne Keothavong (GBR) & Conchita Martinez (ESP)	Iva Majoli (CRO) & Magdalena Maleeva (BUL)	Martina Navratilova (USA) & Selima Sfar (TUN)	Wins	Losses	Final
Lindsay Davenport (USA) & Mary Joe Fernandez (USA)		6/3 6/4 W	5/7 6/4 [8-10] L	w/o L	1	2	
Anne Keothavong (GBR) & Conchita Martinez (ESP)	3/6 4/6 L		w/o L	0/6 1/6 L	0	3	Martina Navratilova (USA) & Selima Sfar (TUN)
Iva Majoli (CRO) & Magdalena Maleeva (BUL)	7/5 4/6 [10-8] W	w/o W		3/6 4/6 L	2	1	
Martina Navratilova (USA) & Selima Sfar (TUN)	w/o W	6/0 6/1 W	6/3 6/4 W		3	0	

GROUP B	Tracy Austin (USA) & Helena Sukova (CZE)	Andrea Jaeger (USA) & Rennae Stubbs (AUS)	Jana Novotna (CZE) & Barbara Schett (AUT)	Nathalie Tauziat (FRA) & Andrea Temesvari (HUN)	Wins	Losses	Final
Tracy Austin (USA) & Helena Sukova (CZE)		6/4 6/4 W	7/6(5) 2/2 Ret'd L	7/5 6/2 W	2	1	
Andrea Jaeger (USA) & Rennae Stubbs (AUS)	4/6 4/6 L		2/6 4/6 L	7/5 6/2 W	1	2	Jana Novotna (CZE) & Barbara Schett (AUT)
Jana Novotna (CZE) & Barbara Schett (AUT)	6/7(5) 2/2 Ret'd W	6/2 6/4 W		6/4 6/2 W	3	0	
Nathalie Tauziat (FRA) & Andrea Temesvari (HUN)	5/7 2/6 L	5/7 2/6 L	4/6 2/6 L		0	3	

Final result: Jana Novotna & Barbara Schett — 6/0 7/6(1)

This event will be played on a 'round robin' basis. Eight invited pairs have been divided into two groups of four and each pair in each group will play one another. The pairs winning most matches will be the champions of their respective groups and will play each other in the final as indicated above. If matches should be equal in any group, the head-to-head result between the two pairs with the same number of wins will determine the winning pair of the group.

EVENT XIII – THE WHEELCHAIR GENTLEMEN'S DOUBLES 2013
Holders: STEPHANE HOUDET (FRA) & SHINGO KUNIEDA (JPN)

The Champions will become the holders, for one year only, of a Cup presented by The All England Lawn and Croquet Club. The Champions will receive a Silver Salver. The Runners-up will each receive a Silver Medal. The matches will be the best of three tie-break sets.

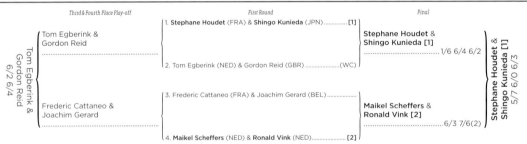

Heavy type denotes seeded players. The figure in brackets against names denotes the order in which they have been seeded.

EVENT XIV – THE WHEELCHAIR LADIES' DOUBLES 2013
Holders: JISKE GRIFFIOEN (NED) & ANIEK VAN KOOT (NED)

The Champions will become the holders, for one year only, of a Cup presented by The All England Lawn and Croquet Club. The Champions will receive a Silver Salver. The Runners-up will each receive a Silver Medal. The matches will be the best of three tie-break sets.

Heavy type denotes seeded players. The figure in brackets against names denotes the order in which they have been seeded.

ROLLS OF HONOUR
GENTLEMEN'S SINGLES CHAMPIONS & RUNNERS-UP

1877	S.W.Gore *W.C.Marshall*	1903	H.L.Doherty *F.L.Riseley*	1933	J.H.Crawford *H.E.Vines*	1965	R.S.Emerson *F.S.Stolle*	1991	M.D.Stich *B.F.Becker*
1878	P.F.Hadow *S.W.Gore*	1904	H.L.Doherty *F.L.Riseley*	1934	F.J.Perry *J.H.Crawford*	1966	M.M.Santana *R.D.Ralston*	1992	A.K.Agassi *G.S.Ivanisevic*
* 1879	J.T.Hartley *V.T.St.L.Goold*	1905	H.L.Doherty *N.E.Brookes*	1935	F.J.Perry *G.von Cramm*	1967	J.D.Newcombe *W.P.Bungert*	1993	P.Sampras *J.S.Courier*
1880	J.T.Hartley *H.F.Lawford*	1906	H.L.Doherty *F.L.Riseley*	1936	F.J.Perry *G.von Cramm*	1968	R.G.Laver *A.D.Roche*	1994	P.Sampras *G.S.Ivanisevic*
1881	W.C.Renshaw *J.T.Hartley*	* 1907	N.E.Brookes *A.W.Gore*	* 1937	J.D.Budge *G.von Cramm*	1969	R.G.Laver *J.D.Newcombe*	1995	P.Sampras *B.F.Becker*
1882	W.C.Renshaw *J.E.Renshaw*	* 1908	A.W.Gore *H.R.Barrett*	1938	J.D.Budge *H.W.Austin*	1970	J.D.Newcombe *K.R.Rosewall*	1996	R.P.S.Krajicek *M.O.Washington*
1883	W.C.Renshaw *J.E.Renshaw*	1909	A.W.Gore *M.J.G.Ritchie*	* 1939	R.L.Riggs *E.T.Cooke*	1971	J.D.Newcombe *S.R.Smith*	1997	P.Sampras *C.A.Pioline*
1884	W.C.Renshaw *H.F.Lawford*	1910	A.F.Wilding *A.W.Gore*	* 1946	Y.F.M.Petra *G.E.Brown*	* 1972	S.R.Smith *I.Nastase*	1998	P.Sampras *G.S.Ivanisevic*
1885	W.C.Renshaw *H.F.Lawford*	1911	A.F.Wilding *H.R.Barrett*	1947	J.A.Kramer *T.P.Brown*	* 1973	J.Kodes *A.Metreveli*	1999	P.Sampras *A.K.Agassi*
1886	W.C.Renshaw *H.F.Lawford*	1912	A.F.Wilding *A.W.Gore*	* 1948	R.Falkenburg *J.E.Bromwich*	1974	J.S.Connors *K.R.Rosewall*	2000	P.Sampras *P.M.Rafter*
* 1887	H.F.Lawford *J.E.Renshaw*	1913	A.F.Wilding *M.E.McLoughlin*	1949	F.R.Schroeder *J.Drobny*	1975	A.R.Ashe *J.S.Connors*	2001	G.Ivanisevic *P.M.Rafter*
1888	J.E.Renshaw *H.F.Lawford*	1914	N.E.Brookes *A.F.Wilding*	* 1950	J.E.Patty *F.A.Sedgman*	1976	B.R.Borg *I.Nastase*	2002	L.G.Hewitt *D.P.Nalbandian*
1889	W.C.Renshaw *J.E.Renshaw*	1919	G.L.Patterson *N.E.Brookes*	1951	R.Savitt *K.B.McGregor*	1977	B.R.Borg *J.S.Connors*	2003	R.Federer *M.A.Philippoussis*
1890	W.J.Hamilton *W.C.Renshaw*	1920	W.T.Tilden *G.L.Patterson*	1952	F.A.Sedgman *J.Drobny*	1978	B.R.Borg *J.S.Connors*	2004	R.Federer *A.S.Roddick*
* 1891	W.Baddeley *J.Pim*	1921	W.T.Tilden *B.I.C.Norton*	* 1953	E.V.Seixas *K.Nielsen*	1979	B.R.Borg *L.R.Tanner*	2005	R.Federer *A.S.Roddick*
1892	W.Baddeley *J.Pim*	*† 1922	G.L.Patterson *R.Lycett*	1954	J.Drobny *K.R.Rosewall*	1980	B.Borg *J.P.McEnroe*	2006	R.Federer *R.Nadal*
1893	J.Pim *W.Baddeley*	* 1923	W.M.Johnston *F.T.Hunter*	1955	M.A.Trabert *K.Nielsen*	1981	J.P.McEnroe *B.R.Borg*	2007	R.Federer *R.Nadal*
1894	J.Pim *W.Baddeley*	* 1924	J.R.Borotra *J.R.Lacoste*	* 1956	L.A.Hoad *K.R.Rosewall*	1982	J.S.Connors *J.P.McEnroe*	2008	R.Nadal *R.Federer*
* 1895	W.Baddeley *W.V.Eaves*	1925	J.R.Lacoste *J.R.Borotra*	1957	L.A.Hoad *A.J.Cooper*	1983	J.P.McEnroe *C.J.Lewis*	2009	R.Federer *A.S.Roddick*
1896	H.S.Mahony *W.Baddeley*	* 1926	J.R.Borotra *H.O.Kinsey*	* 1958	A.J.Cooper *N.A.Fraser*	1984	J.P.McEnroe *J.S.Connors*	2010	R.Nadal *T.Berdych*
1897	R.F.Doherty *H.S.Mahony*	1927	H.J.Cochet *J.R.Borotra*	* 1959	A.R.Olmedo *R.G.Laver*	1985	B.F.Becker *K.M.Curren*	2011	N.Djokovic *R.Nadal*
1898	R.F.Doherty *H.L.Doherty*	1928	J.R.Lacoste *H.J.Cochet*	* 1960	N.A.Fraser *R.G.Laver*	1986	B.F.Becker *I.Lendl*	2012	R.Federer *A.Murray*
1899	R.F.Doherty *A.W.Gore*	* 1929	H.J.Cochet *J.R.Borotra*	1961	R.G.Laver *C.R.McKinley*	1987	P.H.Cash *I.Lendl*	2013	A.Murray *N.Djokovic*
1900	R.F.Doherty *S.H.Smith*	1930	W.T.Tilden *W.L.Allison*	1962	R.G.Laver *M.F.Mulligan*	1988	S.B.Edberg *B.F.Becker*	2014	N.Djokovic *R.Federer*
1901	A.W.Gore *R.F.Doherty*	* 1931	S.B.B.Wood *F.X.Shields*	* 1963	C.R.McKinley *F.S.Stolle*	1989	B.F.Becker *S.B.Edberg*		
1902	H.L.Doherty *A.W.Gore*	1932	H.E.Vines *H.W.Austin*	1964	R.S.Emerson *F.S.Stolle*	1990	S.B.Edberg *B.F.Becker*		

For the years 1913, 1914 and 1919-1923 inclusive the above records include the "World's Championships on Grass" granted to The Lawn Tennis Association by The International Lawn Tennis Federation.

This title was then abolished and commencing in 1924 they became The Official Lawn Tennis Championships recognised by The International Lawn Tennis Federation.

Prior to 1922 the holders in the Singles Events and Gentlemen's Doubles did not compete in The Championships but met the winners of these events in the Challenge Rounds.

† Challenge Round abolished: holders subsequently played through.

* The holder did not defend the title.

LADIES' SINGLES CHAMPIONS & RUNNERS-UP

1884 Miss M.E.E.Watson *Miss L.M.Watson*	1910 Mrs.R.L.Chambers *Miss P.D.H.Boothby*	*1946 Miss P.M.Betz *Miss A.L.Brough*	1972 Mrs.L.W.King *Miss E.F.Goolagong*
1885 Miss M.E.E.Watson *Miss B.Bingley*	1911 Mrs.R.L.Chambers *Miss P.D.H.Boothby*	*1947 Miss M.E.Osborne *Miss D.J.Hart*	1973 Mrs.L.W.King *Miss C.M.Evert*
1886 Miss B.Bingley *Miss M.E.E.Watson*	*1912 Mrs.D.T.R.Larcombe *Mrs.A.Sterry*	1948 Miss A.L.Brough *Miss D.J.Hart*	1974 Miss C.M.Evert *Mrs.O.V.Morozova*
1887 Miss C.Dod *Miss B.Bingley*	*1913 Mrs.R.L.Chambers *Mrs.R.J.McNair*	1949 Miss A.L.Brough *Mrs.W.du Pont*	1975 Mrs.L.W.King *Mrs.R.A.Cawley*
1888 Miss C.Dod *Mrs.G.W.Hillyard*	1914 Mrs.R.L.Chambers *Mrs.D.T.R.Larcombe*	1950 Miss A.L.Brough *Mrs.W.du Pont*	*1976 Miss C.M.Evert *Mrs.R.A.Cawley*
*1889 Mrs.G.W.Hillyard *Miss H.G.B.Rice*	1919 Miss S.R.F.Lenglen *Mrs.R.L.Chambers*	1951 Miss D.J.Hart *Miss S.J.Fry*	1977 Miss S.V.Wade *Miss B.F.Stove*
*1890 Miss H.G.B.Rice *Miss M.Jacks*	1920 Miss S.R.F.Lenglen *Mrs.R.L.Chambers*	1952 Miss M.C.Connolly *Miss A.L.Brough*	1978 Miss M.Navratilova *Miss C.M.Evert*
*1891 Miss C.Dod *Mrs.G.W.Hillyard*	1921 Miss S.R.F.Lenglen *Miss E.M.Ryan*	1953 Miss M.C.Connolly *Miss D.J.Hart*	1979 Miss M.Navratilova *Mrs.J.M.Lloyd*
1892 Miss C.Dod *Mrs.G.W.Hillyard*	†1922 Miss S.R.F.Lenglen *Mrs.F.I.Mallory*	1954 Miss M.C.Connolly *Miss A.L.Brough*	1980 Mrs.R.A.Cawley *Mrs.J.M.Lloyd*
1893 Miss C.Dod *Mrs.G.W.Hillyard*	1923 Miss S.R.F.Lenglen *Miss K.McKane*	*1955 Miss A.L.Brough *Mrs.J.G.Fleitz*	*1981 Mrs.J.M.Lloyd *Miss H.Mandlikova*
*1894 Mrs.G.W.Hillyard *Miss E.L.Austin*	1924 Miss K.McKane *Miss H.N.Wills*	1956 Miss S.J.Fry *Miss A.Buxton*	1982 Miss M.Navratilova *Mrs.J.M.Lloyd*
*1895 Miss C.R.Cooper *Miss H.Jackson*	1925 Miss S.R.F.Lenglen *Miss J.C.Fry*	*1957 Miss A.Gibson *Miss D.R.Hard*	1983 Miss M.Navratilova *Miss A.Jaeger*
1896 Miss C.R.Cooper *Mrs.W.H.Pickering*	1926 Mrs.L.A.Godfree *Miss E.M.de Alvarez*	1958 Miss A.Gibson *Miss F.A.M.Mortimer*	1984 Miss M.Navratilova *Mrs.J.M.Lloyd*
1897 Mrs.G.W.Hillyard *Miss C.R.Cooper*	1927 Miss H.Wills *Miss E.M.de Alvarez*	*1959 Miss M.E.A.Bueno *Miss D.R.Hard*	1985 Miss M.Navratilova *Mrs.J.M.Lloyd*
*1898 Miss C.R.Cooper *Miss M.L.Martin*	1928 Miss H.N.Wills *Miss E.M.de Alvarez*	1960 Miss M.E.A.Bueno *Miss S.Reynolds*	1986 Miss M.Navratilova *Miss H.Mandlikova*
1899 Mrs.G.W.Hillyard *Miss C.R.Cooper*	1929 Miss H.N.Wills *Miss H.H.Jacobs*	*1961 Miss F.A.M.Mortimer *Miss C.C.Truman*	1987 Miss M.Navratilova *Miss S.M.Graf*
1900 Mrs.G.W.Hillyard *Miss C.R.Cooper*	1930 Mrs.F.S.Moody *Miss E.M.Ryan*	1962 Mrs.J.R.Susman *Mrs.C.Sukova*	1988 Miss S.M.Graf *Miss M.Navratilova*
1901 Mrs.A.Sterry *Mrs.G.W.Hillyard*	*1931 Miss C.Aussem *Miss H.Krahwinkel*	*1963 Miss M.Smith *Miss B.J.Moffitt*	1989 Miss S.M.Graf *Miss M.Navratilova*
1902 Miss M.E.Robb *Mrs.A.Sterry*	*1932 Mrs.F.S.Moody *Miss H.H.Jacobs*	1964 Miss M.E.A.Bueno *Miss M.Smith*	1990 Miss M.Navratilova *Miss Z.L.Garrison*
*1903 Miss D.K.Douglass *Miss E.W.Thomson*	1933 Mrs.F.S.Moody *Miss D.E.Round*	1965 Miss M.Smith *Miss M.E.A.Bueno*	1991 Miss S.M.Graf *Miss G.B.Sabatini*
1904 Miss D.K.Douglass *Mrs.A.Sterry*	*1934 Miss D.E.Round *Miss H.H.Jacobs*	1966 Mrs.L.W.King *Miss M.E.A.Bueno*	1992 Miss S.M.Graf *Miss M.Seles*
1905 Miss M.G.Sutton *Miss D.K.Douglass*	1935 Mrs.F.S.Moody *Miss H.H.Jacobs*	1967 Mrs.L.W.King *Mrs.P.F.Jones*	1993 Miss S.M.Graf *Miss J.Novotna*
1906 Miss D.K.Douglass *Miss M.G.Sutton*	*1936 Miss H.H.Jacobs *Miss S.Sperling*	1968 Mrs.L.W.King *Miss J.A.M.Tegart*	1994 Miss I.C.Martinez *Miss M.Navratilova*
1907 Miss M.G.Sutton *Mrs.R.L.Chambers*	1937 Mrs.D.E.Round *Miss J.Jedrzejowska*	1969 Mrs.P.F.Jones *Mrs.L.W.King*	1995 Miss S.M.Graf *Miss A.I.M.Sanchez Vicario*
*1908 Mrs.A.Sterry *Miss A.M.Morton*	*1938 Mrs.F.S.Moody *Miss H.H.Jacobs*	*1970 Mrs.B.M.Court *Mrs.L.W.King*	1996 Miss S.M.Graf *Miss A.I.M.Sanchez Vicario*
*1909 Miss P.D.H.Boothby *Miss A.M.Morton*	*1939 Miss A.Marble *Miss K.E.Stammers*	1971 Miss E.F.Goolagong *Mrs.B.M.Court*	

*1997 Miss M.Hingis *Miss J.Novotna*
1998 Miss J.Novotna *Miss N.Tauziat*
1999 Miss L.A.Davenport *Miss S.M.Graf*
2000 Miss V.E.S.Williams *Miss L.A.Davenport*
2001 Miss V.E.S.Williams *Miss J.Henin*
2002 Miss S.J.Williams *Miss V.E.S.Williams*
2003 Miss S.J.Williams *Miss V.E.S.Williams*
2004 Miss M.Sharapova *Miss S.J.Williams*
2005 Miss V.E.S.Williams *Miss L.A.Davenport*
2006 Miss A.Mauresmo *Mrs J.Henin-Hardenne*
2007 Miss V.E.S.Williams *Miss M.S.Bartoli*
2008 Miss V.E.S.Williams *Miss S.J.Williams*
2009 Miss S.J.Williams *Miss V.E.S.Williams*
2010 Miss S.J.Williams *Miss V.Zvonareva*
2011 Miss P.Kvitova *Miss M.Sharapova*
2012 Miss S.J.Williams *Miss A.R.Radwanska*
2013 Miss M.S.Bartoli *Miss S.Lisicki*
2014 Miss P.Kvitova *Miss E.Bouchard*

MAIDEN NAMES OF LADIES' CHAMPIONS (In the tables the following have been recorded in both married and single identities)

Mrs R. Cawley	Miss E. F. Goolagong	Mrs. G. W. Hillyard	Miss B. Bingley	Mrs. G. E. Reid	Miss K. Melville
Mrs. R. L. Chambers	Miss D. K. Douglass	Mrs. P. F. Jones	Miss A. S. Haydon	Mrs. P. D. Smylie	Miss E. M. Sayers
Mrs. B. M. Court	Miss M. Smith	Mrs. L. W. King	Miss B. J. Moffitt	Frau S. Sperling	Fraulein H Krahwinkel
Mrs. B. C. Covell	Miss P. L. Howkins	Mrs. M. R. King	Miss P. E. Mudford	Mrs A. Sterry	Miss C. Cooper
Mrs. D. E. Dalton	Miss J. A. M. Tegart	Mrs. D. R. Larcombe	Miss E. W. Thomson	Mrs. J. R. Susman	Miss K. Hantze
Mrs. W. du Pont	Miss M. Osborne	Mrs. J. M. Lloyd	Miss C. M. Evert		
Mrs. L. A. Godfree	Miss K. McKane	Mrs. F. S. Moody	Miss H. Wills		
Mrs. H. F. Gourlay Cawley	Miss H. F. Gourlay	Mrs. O. Morozova	Miss O. Morozova		
Mrs. Henin-Hardenne	Miss J. Henin	Mrs. L. E. G. Price	Miss S. Reynolds		

GENTLEMEN'S DOUBLES CHAMPIONS & RUNNERS-UP

Year	Champions / Runners-up

1879 L.R.Erskine and H.F.Lawford
F.Durant and G.E.Tabor

1880 W.C.Renshaw and J.E.Renshaw
O.E.Woodhouse and C.J.Cole

1881 W.C.Renshaw and J.E.Renshaw
W.J.Down and H.Vaughan

1882 J.T.Hartley and R.T.Richardson
J.G.Horn and C.B.Russell

1883 C.W.Grinstead and C.E.Welldon
C.B.Russell and R.T.Milford

1884 W.C.Renshaw and J.E.Renshaw
E.W.Lewis and E.L.Williams

1885 W.C.Renshaw and J.E.Renshaw
C.E.Farrer and A.J.Stanley

1886 W.C.Renshaw and J.E.Renshaw
C.E.Farrer and A.J.Stanley

1887 P.B.Lyon and H.W.W.Wilberforce
J.H.Crispe and E.Barratt Smith

1888 W.C.Renshaw and J.E.Renshaw
P B.Lyon and H.W.W.Wilberforce

1889 W.C.Renshaw and J.E.Renshaw
E.W.Lewis and G.W.Hillyard

1890 J.Pim and F.O.Stoker
E.W.Lewis and G.W.Hillyard

1891 W.Baddeley and H.Baddeley
J.Pim and F.O.Stoker

1892 H.S.Barlow and E.W.Lewis
W.Baddeley and H.Baddeley

1893 J.Pim and F.O.Stoker
E.W.Lewis and H.S.Barlow

1894 W.Baddeley and H.Baddeley
H.S.Barlow and C.H.Martin

1895 W.Baddeley and H.Baddeley
E.W.Lewis and W.V.Eaves

1896 W.Baddeley and H.Baddeley
R.F.Doherty and H.A.Nisbet

1897 R.F.Doherty and H.L.Doherty
W.Baddeley and H.Baddeley

1898 R.F.Doherty and H.L .Doherty
H.A.Nisbet and C.Hobart

1899 R.F.Doherty and H.L.Doherty
H.A.Nisbet and C.Hobart

1900 R.F.Doherty and H.L.Doherty
H.R.Barrett and H.A.Nisbet

1901 R.F.Doherty and H.L.Doherty
D.Davis and H.Ward

1902 S.H.Smith and F.L.Riseley
R.F.Doherty and H.L.Doherty

1903 R.F.Doherty and H.L.Doherty
S.H.Smith and F.L.Riseley

1904 R.F.Doherty and H.L.Doherty
S.H.Smith and F.L.Riseley

1905 R.F.Doherty and H.L.Doherty
S.H.Smith and F.L.Riseley

1906 S.H.Smith and F.L.Riseley
R.F.Doherty and H.L.Doherty

1907 N.E.Brookes and A.F.Wilding
B.C.Wright and K.Behr

1908 A.F.Wilding and M.J.G.Ritchie
A.W.Gore and H.R.Barrett

1909 A.W.Gore and H.R.Barrett
S.N.Doust and H.A.Parker

1910 A.F.Wilding and M.J.G.Ritchie
A.W.Gore and H.R.Barrett

1911 M.O.Decugis and A.H.Gobert
M.J.G.Ritchie and A.F.Wilding

1912 H.R.Barrett and C.P.Dixon
M.O.Decugis and A.H.Gobert

1913 H.R.Barrett and C.P.Dixon
F.W.Rahe and H.Kleinschroth

1914 N.E.Brookes and A.F.Wilding
H.R.Barrett and C.P.Dixon

1919 R.V.Thomas and P.O.Wood
R.Lycett and R.W.Heath

1920 R.N.Williams and C.S.Garland
A.R.F.Kingscote and J.C.Parke

1921 R.Lycett and M.Woosnam
F.G.Lowe and A.H.Lowe

1922 R.Lycett and J.O.Anderson
G.L.Patterson and P.O.Wood

1923 R.Lycett and L.A.Godfree
Count M. de Gomar and E.Flaquer

1924 F.T.Hunter and V.Richards
R.N.Williams and W.M.Washburn

1925 J.R.Borotra and R.Lacoste
J.F.Hennessey and R.J.Casey

1926 H.J.Cochet and J.Brugnon
V.Richards and H.O.Kinsey

1927 F.T.Hunter and W.T.Tilden
J.Brugnon and H.J.Cochet

1928 H.J.Cochet and J.Brugnon
G.L.Patterson and J.B.Hawkes

1929 W.L.Allison and J.W.Van Ryn
J.C.Gregory and I.G.Collins

1930 W.L.Allison and J.W.Van Ryn
J.T.G.H.Doeg and G.M.Lott

1931 G.M Lott and J.W.Van Ryn
H.J.Cochet and J.Brugnon

1932 J.R.Borotra and J.Brugnon
G.P.Hughes and F.J.Perry

1933 J.R.Borotra and J.Brugnon
R.Nunoi and J.Satoh

1934 G.M.Lott and L.R.Stoefen
J.R.Borotra and J.Brugnon

1935 J.H.Crawford and A.K.Quist
W.L.Allison and J.W.Van Ryn

1936 G.P.Hughes and C.R.D.Tuckey
C.E.Hare and F.H.D.Wilde

1937 J.D.Budge and G.C.Mako
G.P.Hughes and C.R.D.Tuckey

1938 J.D.Budge and G.C.Mako
H.E.O.Henkel and G.von Metaxa

1939 R.L.Riggs and E.T.Cooke
C.E.Hare and F.H.D.Wilde

1946 T.P.Brown and J.A.Kramer
G.E.Brown and D.R.Pails

1947 R.Falkenburg and J.A.Kramer
A.J.Mottram and O.W.T.Sidwell

1948 J.E.Bromwich and F.A.Sedgman
T.P.Brown and G.P.Mulloy

1949 R.A.Gonzales and F.A.Parker
G.P.Mulloy and F.R.Schroeder

1950 J.E.Bromwich and A.K.Quist
G.E.Brown and O.W.T.Sidwell

1951 K.B.McGregor and F.A.Sedgman
J.Drobny and E.W.Sturgess

1952 K.B.McGregor and F.A.Sedgman
E.V.Seixas and E.W.Sturgess

1953 L.A.Hoad and K.R.Rosewall
R.N.Hartwig and M.G.Rose

1954 R.N.Hartwig and M.G.Rose
E.V.Seixas and M.A.Trabert

1955 R.N.Hartwig and L.A.Hoad
N.A.Fraser and K.R.Rosewall

1956 L.A.Hoad and K.R.Rosewall
N.Pietrangeli and O.Sirola

1957 G.P.Mulloy and J.E.Patty
N.A.Fraser and L.A.Hoad

1958 S.V.Davidson and U.C.J.Schmidt
A.J.Cooper and N.A.Fraser

1959 R.S.Emerson and N.A.Fraser
R.G.Laver and R.Mark

1960 R.H.Osuna and R.D.Ralston
M.G.Davies and R.K.Wilson

1961 R.S.Emerson and N.A.Fraser
R.A.J.Hewitt and F.S.Stolle

1962 R.A.J.Hewitt and F.S.Stolle
B.Jovanovic and N.Pilic

1963 R.H.Osuna and A.Palafox
J.C.Barclay and P.Darmon

1964 R.A.J.Hewitt and F.S.Stolle
R.S.Emerson and K.N.Fletcher

1965 J.D.Newcombe and A.D.Roche
K.N.Fletcher and R.A.J.Hewitt

1966 K.N.Fletcher and J.D.Newcombe
W.W.Bowrey and O.K.Davidson

1967 R.A.J.Hewitt and F.D.McMillan
R.S.Emerson and K.N.Fletcher

1968 J.D.Newcombe and A.D.Roche
K.R.Rosewall and F.S.Stolle

1969 J.D.Newcombe and A.D.Roche
T.S.Okker and M.C.Reissen

1970 J.D.Newcombe and A.D.Roche
K.R.Rosewall and F.S.Stolle

1971 R.S.Emerson and R.G.Laver
A.R.Ashe and R.D.Ralston

1972 R.A.J.Hewitt and F.D.McMillan
S.R.Smith and E.J.van Dillen

1973 J.S.Connors and I.Nastase
J.R.Cooper and N.A.Fraser

1974 J.D.Newcombe and A.D.Roche
R.C.Lutz and S.R.Smith

1975 V.K.Gerulaitis and A.Mayer
C.Dowdeswell and A.J.Stone

1976 B.E.Gottfried and R.C.Ramirez
R.L.Case and G.Masters

1977 R.L.Case and G.Masters
J.G.Alexander and P.C.Dent

1978 R.A.J.Hewitt and F.D.McMillan
P.B.Fleming and J.P.McEnroe

1979 P.B.Fleming and J.P.McEnroe
B.E.Gottfried and R.C.Ramirez

1980 P.McNamara and P.F.McNamee
R.C.Lutz and S.R.Smith

1981 P.B.Fleming and J.P.McEnroe
R.C.Lutz and S.R.Smith

1982 P.McNamara and P.F.McNamee
P.B.Fleming and J.P.McEnroe

1983 P.B.Fleming and J.P.McEnroe
T.E.Gullikson and T.R.Gullikson

1984 P.B.Fleming and J.P.McEnroe
P.Cash and P.McNamee

1985 H.P.Guenthardt and B.Taroczy
P.H.Cash and J.B.Fitzgerald

1986 T.K.Nystrom and M.A.O.Wilander
G.W.Donnelly and P.B.Fleming

1987 K.E.Flach and R.A.Seguso
S.Casal and E.Sanchez

1988 K.E.Flach and R.A.Seguso
J.B.Fitzgerald and A.P.Jarryd

1989 J.B.Fitzgerald and A.P.Jarryd
R.D.Leach and J.R.Pugh

1990 R.D.Leach and J.R.Pugh
P.Aldrich and D.T.Visser

1991 J.B.Fitzgerald and A.P.Jarryd
J.A.Frana and L.Lavalle

1992 J.P.McEnroe and M.D.Stich
J.F.Grabb and R.A.Reneberg

1993 T.A.Woodbridge and M.R.Woodforde
G.D.Connell and P.J.Galbraith

1994 T.A.Woodbridge and M.R.Woodforde
G.D.Connell and P.J.Galbraith

1995 T.A.Woodbridge and M.R.Woodforde
R.D.Leach and S.D.Melville

1996 T.A.Woodbridge and M.R.Woodforde
B.H.Black and G.D.Connell

1997 T.A.Woodbridge and M.R.Woodforde
J.F.Eltingh and P.V.N.Haarhuis

1998 J.F.Eltingh and P.V.N.Haarhuis
T.A.Woodbridge and M.R.Woodforde

1999 M.S.Bhupathi and L.A.Paes
P.V.NHaarhuis and J.E.Palmer

2000 T.A.Woodbridge and M.R.Woodforde
P.V.N.Haarhuis and S.F.Stolle

2001 D.J.Johnson and J.E.Palmer
J.Novak and D.Rikl

2002 J.L.Bjorkman and T.A Woodbridge
M.S.Knowles and D.M.Nestor

2003 J.L.Bjorkman and T.A Woodbridge
M.S.Bhupathi and M.N.Mirnyi

2004 J.L.Bjorkman and T.A Woodbridge
J.Knowle and N.Zimonjic

2005 S.W.I.Huss and W.A.Moodie
R.C.Bryan and M.C.Bryan

2006 R.C.Bryan and M.C.Bryan
F.V.Santoro and N.Zimonjic

2007 A.Clement and M.Llodra
R.C.Bryan and M.C.Bryan

2008 D.M.Nestor and N.Zimonjic
J.L.Bjorkman and K.R.Ullyett

2009 D.M.Nestor and N.Zimonjic
R.C.Bryan and M.C.Bryan

2010 J.Melzer and P.Petzschner
R.S.Lindstedt and H.V.Tecau

2011 R.C.Bryan and M.C.Bryan
R.S.Lindstedt and H.V.Tecau

2012 J.F.Marray and F.L.Nielsen
R.S.Lindstedt and H.V.Tecau

2013 R.C.Bryan and M.C.Bryan
I.Dodig and M.Melo

2014 V.Pospisil and J.Sock
R.C.Bryan and M.C.Bryan

LADIES' DOUBLES CHAMPIONS & RUNNERS-UP

1913	Mrs.R.J.McNair and Miss P.D.H.Boothby *Mrs.A.Sterry and Mrs.R.L.Chambers*
1914	Miss E.M.Ryan and Miss A.M.Morton *Mrs.D.T.R.Larcombe and Mrs.F.J.Hannam*
1919	Miss S.R.F.Lenglen and Miss E.M.Ryan *Mrs.R.L.Chambers and Mrs.D.T.R.Larcombe*
1920	Miss S.R.F.Lenglen and Miss E.M.Ryan *Mrs.R.L.Chambers and Mrs.D.T.R.Larcombe*
1921	Miss S.R.F.Lenglen and Miss E.M.Ryan *Mrs.A.E.Beamish and Mrs.G.E.Peacock*
1922	Miss S.R.F.Lenglen and Miss E.M.Ryan *Mrs.A.D.Stocks and Miss K.McKane*
1923	Miss S.R.F.Lenglen and Miss E.M.Ryan *Miss J.W.Austin and Miss E.L.Colyer*
1924	Mrs.G.Wightman and Miss H.Wills *Mrs.B.C.Covell and Miss K.McKane*
1925	Miss S.Lenglen and Miss E.Ryan *Mrs.A.V.Bridge and Mrs.C.G.McIlquham*
1926	Miss E.M.Ryan and Miss M.K.Browne *Mrs.L.A.Godfree and Miss E.L.Colyer*
1927	Miss H.N.Wills and Miss E.M.Ryan *Miss E.L.Heine and Mrs.G.E.Peacock*
1928	Mrs.M.R.Watson and Miss M.A.Saunders *Miss E.H.Harvey and Miss E.Bennett*
1929	Mrs.M.R.Watson and Mrs.L.R.C.Michell *Mrs.B.C.Covell and Mrs.W.P.Barron*
1930	Mrs.F.S.Moody and Miss E.M.Ryan *Miss E.A.Cross and Miss S.H.Palfrey*
1931	Mrs.W.P.Barron and Miss P.E.Mudford *Miss D.E.Metaxa and Miss J.Sigart*
1932	Miss D.E.Metaxa and Miss J.Sigart *Miss E.M.Ryan and Miss H.H.Jacobs*
1933	Mrs.R.Mathieu and Miss E.M.Ryan *Miss W.A.James and Miss A.M.Yorke*
1934	Mrs.R.Mathieu and Miss E.M.Ryan *Mrs.D.B.Andrus and Mrs.C.F.Henrotin*
1935	Miss W.A.James and Miss K.E.Stammers *Mrs.R.Mathieu and Mrs.S.Sperling*
1936	Miss W.A.James and Miss K.E.Stammers *Mrs.M.Fabyan and Miss H.H.Jacobs*
1937	Mrs.R.Mathieu and Miss A.M.Yorke *Mrs.M.R.King and Mrs.J.B.Pittman*
1938	Mrs.M.Fabyan and Miss A.Marble *Mrs.R.Mathieu and Miss A.M.Yorke*
1939	Mrs.M.Fabyan and Miss A.Marble *Miss H.H.Jacobs and Miss A.M.Yorke*
1946	Miss A.L.Brough and Miss M.E.Osborne *Miss P.M.Betz and Miss D.J.Hart*
1947	Miss D.J.Hart and Mrs.R.B.Todd *Miss A.L.Brough and Miss M.E.Osborne*
1948	Miss A.L.Brough and Mrs.W.du Pont *Miss D.J.Hart and Mrs.R.B.Todd*
1949	Miss A.L.Brough and Mrs.W.du Pont *Miss G.Moran and Mrs.R.B.Todd*
1950	Miss A.L.Brough and Mrs.W.du Pont *Miss S.J.Fry and Miss D.J.Hart*
1951	Miss S.J.Fry and Miss D.J.Hart *Miss A.L.Brough and Mrs.W.du Pont*
1952	Miss S.J.Fry and Miss D.J.Hart *Miss A.L.Brough and Miss M.C.Connolly*
1953	Miss S.J.Fry and Miss D.J.Hart *Miss M.C.Connolly and Miss J.A.Sampson*
1954	Miss A.L.Brough and Mrs.W.du Pont *Miss S.J.Fry and Miss D.J.Hart*
1955	Miss F.A.Mortimer and Miss J.A.Shilcock *Miss S.J.Bloomer and Miss P.E.Ward*
1956	Miss A.Buxton and Miss A.Gibson *Miss E.F.Muller and Miss D.G.Seeney*
1957	Miss A.Gibson and Miss D.R.Hard *Mrs.K.Hawton and Mrs.M.N.Long*
1958	Miss M.E.A.Bueno and Miss A.Gibson *Mrs.W.du Pont and Miss M.Varner*
1959	Miss J.Arth and Miss D.R.Hard *Mrs.J.G.Fleitz and Miss C.C.Truman*
1960	Miss M.E.A.Bueno and Miss D.R.Hard *Miss S.Reynolds and Miss R.Schuurman*
1961	Miss K.J.Hantze and Miss B.J.Moffitt *Miss J.P.Lehane and Miss M.Smith*
1962	Miss B.J.Moffitt and Mrs.J.R.Susman *Mrs.L.E.G.Price and Miss R.Schuurman*
1963	Miss M.E.A.Bueno and Miss D.R.Hard *Miss R.A.Ebbern and Miss M.Smith*
1964	Miss M.Smith and Miss L.R.Turner *Miss B.J.Moffitt and Mrs.J.R.Susman*
1965	Miss M.E.A.Bueno and Miss B.J.Moffitt *Miss F.G.Durr and Miss J.P.Lieffrig*
1966	Miss M.E.A.Bueno and Miss N.A.Richey *Miss M.Smith and Miss J.A.M.Tegart*
1967	Miss R.Casals and Mrs.L.W.King *Miss M.E.A.Bueno and Miss N.A.Richey*
1968	Miss R.Casals and Mrs.L.W.King *Miss F.G.Durr and Mrs.P.F.Jones*
1969	Mrs.B.M.Court and Miss J.A.M.Tegart *Miss P.S.A.Hogan and Miss M.Michel*
1970	Miss R.Casals and Mrs.L.W.King *Miss F.G.Durr and Miss S.V.Wade*
1971	Miss R.Casals and Mrs.L.W.King *Mrs.B.M.Court and Miss E.F.Goolagong*
1972	Mrs.L.W.King and Miss B.F.Stove *Mrs.D.E.Dalton and Miss F.G.Durr*
1973	Miss R.Casals and Mrs.L.W.King *Miss F.G.Durr and Miss B.F.Stove*
1974	Miss E.F.Goolagong and Miss M.Michel *Miss H.F.Gourlay and Miss K.M.Krantzcke*
1975	Miss A.K.Kiyomura and Miss K.Sawamatsu *Miss F.G.Durr and Miss B.F.Stove*
1976	Miss C.M.Evert and Miss M.Navratilova *Mrs.L.W.King and Miss B.F.Stove*
1977	Mrs.R.L.Cawley and Miss J.C.Russell *Miss M.Navratilova and Miss B.F.Stove*
1978	Mrs.G.E.Reid and Miss W.M.Turnbull *Miss M.Jausovec and Miss V.Ruzici*
1979	Mrs.L.W.King and Miss M.Navratilova *Miss B.F.Stove and Miss W.M.Turnbull*
1980	Miss K.Jordan and Miss A.E.Smith *Miss R.Casals and Miss W.M.Turnbull*
1981	Miss M.Navratilova and Miss P.H.Shriver *Miss K.Jordan and Miss A.E.Smith*
1982	Miss M.Navratilova and Miss P.H.Shriver *Miss K.Jordan and Miss A.E.Smith*
1983	Miss M.Navratilova and Miss P.H.Shriver *Miss R.Casals and Miss W.M.Turnbull*
1984	Miss M.Navratilova and Miss P.H.Shriver *Miss K.Jordan and Miss A.E.Smith*
1985	Miss K.Jordan and Mrs.P.D.Smylie *Miss M.Navratilova and Miss P.H.Shriver*
1986	Miss M.Navratilova and Miss P.H.Shriver *Miss H.Mandlikova and Miss W.M.Turnbull*
1987	Miss C.G.Kohde-Kilsch and Miss H.Sukova *Miss H.E.Nagelsen and Mrs.P.D.Smylie*
1988	Miss S.M.Graf and Miss G.B.Sabatini *Miss L.I.Savchenko and Miss N.M.Zvereva*
1989	Miss J.Novotna and Miss H.Sukova *Miss L.I.Savchenko and Miss N.M.Zvereva*
1990	Miss J.Novotna and Miss H.Sukova *Miss K.Jordan and Mrs.P.D.Smylie*
1991	Miss L.I.Savchenko and Miss N.M.Zvereva *Miss B.C.Fernandez and Miss J.Novotna*
1992	Miss B.C.Fernandez and Miss N.M.Zvereva *Miss J.Novotna and Mrs.A.Neiland*
1993	Miss B.C.Fernandez and Miss N.M.Zvereva *Mrs.A.Neiland and Miss J.Novotna*
1994	Miss B.C.Fernandez and Miss N.M.Zvereva *Miss J.Novotna and Miss A.I.M.Sanchez Vicario*
1995	Miss J.Novotna and Miss A.I.M.Sanchez Vicario *Miss B.C.Fernandez and Miss N.M.Zvereva*
1996	Miss M.Hingis and Miss H.Sukova *Miss M.J.McGrath and Mrs.A.Neiland*
1997	Miss B.C.Fernandez and Miss N.M.Zvereva *Miss N.J.Arendt and Miss M.M.Bollegraf*
1998	Miss M.Hingis and Miss J.Novotna *Miss L.A.Davenport and Miss N.M.Zvereva*
1999	Miss L.A.Davenport and Miss C.M.Morariu *Miss M.de Swardt and Miss E.Tatarkova*
2000	Miss S.J.Williams and Miss V.E.S.Williams *Mrs.A.Decugis and Miss A.Sugiyama*
2001	Miss L.M.Raymond and Miss R.P.Stubbs *Miss K.Clijsters and Miss A.Sugiyama*
2002	Miss S.J.Williams and Miss V.E.S.Williams *Miss V.Ruano Pascual and Miss P.L.Suarez*
2003	Miss K.Clijsters and Miss A.Sugiyama *Miss V.Ruano Pascual and Miss P.L.Suarez*
2004	Miss C.C.Black and Miss R.P.Stubbs *Mrs.A.Huber and Miss A.Sugiyama*
2005	Miss C.C.Black and Mrs.A.Huber *Miss S.Kuznetsova and Miss A.Muresmo*
2006	Miss Z.Yan and Miss J.Zheng *Miss V.Ruano Pascual and Miss P.L.Suarez*
2007	Miss C.C.Black and Mrs.A.Huber *Miss K.Srebotnik and Miss A.Sugiyama*
2008	Miss S.J.Williams and Miss V.E.S.Williams *Miss L.M.Raymond and Miss S.J.Stosur*
2009	Miss S.J.Williams and Miss V.E.S.Williams *Miss S.J.Stosur and Miss R.P.Stubbs*
2010	Miss V.King and Miss Y.V.Shvedova *Miss E.S.Vesnina and Miss V.Zvonareva*
2011	Miss K.Peschke and Miss K.Srebotnik *Miss S.Lisicki and Miss S.J.Stosur*
2012	Miss S.J.Williams and Miss V.E.S.Williams *Miss A.Hlavackova and Miss L.Hradecka*
2013	Miss S-W.Hsieh and Miss S.Peng *Miss A.Barty and Miss C.Dellacqua*
2014	Miss S.Errani and Miss R.Vinci *Miss T.Babos and Miss K.Mladenovic*

MIXED DOUBLES CHAMPIONS & RUNNERS-UP

1913	H.Crisp and Mrs.C.O.Tuckey *J.C.Parke and Mrs.D.T.R.Larcombe*
1914	J.C.Parke and Mrs.D.T.R.Larcombe *A.F.Wilding and Miss M.Broquedis*
1919	R.Lycett and Miss E.M.Ryan *A.D.Prebble and Mrs.R.L.Chambers*
1920	G.L.Patterson and Miss S.R.F.Lenglen *R.Lycett and Miss E.M.Ryan*
1921	R.Lycett and Miss E.M.Ryan *M.Woosnam and Miss P.L.Howkins*
1922	P.O.Wood and Miss S.R.F.Lenglen *R.Lycett and Miss E.M.Ryan*
1923	R.Lycett and Miss E.M.Ryan *L.S.Deane and Mrs.W.P.Barron*
1924	J.B.Gilbert and Miss K.McKane *L.A.Godfree and Mrs.W.P.Barron*
1925	J.Borotra and Miss S.R.F.Lenglen *U.L.de Morpurgo and Miss E.M.Ryan*
1926	L.A.Godfree and Mrs.L.A.Godfree *H.O.Kinsey and Miss M.K.Browne*
1927	F.T.Hunter and Miss E.M.Ryan *L.A.Godfree and Mrs.L.A.Godfree*
1928	P.D.B.Spence and Miss E.M.Ryan *J.H.Crawford and Miss D.J.Akhurst*
1929	F.T.Hunter and Miss H.N.Wills *I.G.Collins and Miss J.C.Fry*
1930	J.H.Crawford and Miss E.M.Ryan *D.D.Prenn and Miss H.Krahwinkel*
1931	G.M.Lott and Mrs.L.A.Harper *I.G.Collins and Miss J.C.Ridley*
1932	E.G.Maier and Miss E.M.Ryan *H.C.Hopman and Miss J.Sigart*
1933	G.von Cramm and Miss H.Krahwinkel *N.G.Farquharson and Miss G.M.Heeley*
1934	R.Miki and Miss D.E.Round *H.W.Austin and Mrs.W.P.Barron*
1935	F.J.Perry and Miss D.E.Round *H.C.Hopman and Mrs.H.C.Hopman*
1936	F.J.Perry and Miss D.E.Round *J.D.Budge and Mrs.M.Fabyan*
1937	J.D.Budge and Miss A.Marble *Y.F.M.Petra and Mrs.R.Mathieu*
1938	J.D.Budge and Miss A.Marble *H.E.O.Henkel and Mrs.M.Fabyan*
1939	R.L.Riggs and Miss A.Marble *F.H.D.Wilde and Miss N.B.Brown*
1946	T.P.Brown and Miss A.L.Brough *G.E.Brown and Miss D.M.Bundy*
1947	J.E.Bromwich and Miss A.L.Brough *C.F.Long and Mrs.G.F.Bolton*
1948	J.E.Bromwich and Miss A.L.Brough *F.A.Sedgman and Miss D.J.Hart*
1949	E.W.Sturgess and Mrs.R.A.Summers *J.E.Bromwich and Miss A.L.Brough*
1950	E.W.Sturgess and Miss A.L.Brough *G.E.Brown and Mrs.R.B.Todd*
1951	F.A.Sedgman and Miss D.J.Hart *M.G.Rose and Mrs.G.F.Bolton*
1952	F.A.Sedgman and Miss D.J.Hart *E.J.Morea and Mrs.M.N.Long*
1953	E.V.Seixas and Miss D.J.Hart *E.J.Morea and Miss S.J.Fry*
1954	E.V.Seixas and Miss D.J.Hart *K.R.Rosewall and Mrs.W.du Pont*
1955	E.V.Seixas and Miss D.J.Hart *E.J.Morea and Miss A.L.Brough*
1956	E.V.Seixas and Miss S.J.Fry *G.P.Mulloy and Miss A.Gibson*
1957	M.G.Rose and Miss D.R.Hard *N.A.Fraser and Miss A.Gibson*
1958	R.N.Howe and Miss L.Coghlan *K.Nielsen and Miss A.Gibson*
1959	R.G.Laver and Miss D.R.Hard *N.A.Fraser and Miss M.E.A.Bueno*
1960	R.G.Laver and Miss D.R.Hard *R.N.Howe and Miss M.E.A.Bueno*
1961	F.S.Stolle and Miss L.R.Turner *R.N.Howe and Miss E.Buding*
1962	N.A.Fraser and Mrs.W.du Pont *R.D.Ralston and Miss A.S.Haydon*
1963	K.N.Fletcher and Miss M.Smith *R.A.J.Hewitt and Miss D.R.Hard*
1964	F.S.Stolle and Miss L.R.Turner *K.N.Fletcher and Miss M.Smith*
1965	K.N.Fletcher and Miss M.Smith *A.D.Roche and Miss J.A.M.Tegart*
1966	K.N.Fletcher and Miss M.Smith *R.D.Ralston amd Mrs.L.W.King*
1967	O.K.Davidson and Mrs.L.W.King *K.N.Fletcher and Miss M.E.A.Bueno*
1968	K.N.Fletcher and Mrs.B.M.Court *A.Metreveli and Miss O.V.Morozova*
1969	F.S.Stolle and Mrs.P.F.Jones *A.D.Roche and Miss J.A.M.Tegart*
1970	I.Nastase and Miss R.Casals *A.Metreveli and Miss O.V.Morozova*
1971	O.K.Davidson and Mrs.L.W.King *M.C.Riessen and Mrs.B.M.Court*
1972	I.Nastase and Miss R.Casals *K.G.Warwick and Miss E.F.Goolagong*
1973	O.K.Davidson and Mrs.L.W.King *R.C.Ramirez and Miss J.S.Newberry*
1974	O.K.Davidson and Mrs.L.W.King *M.J.Farrell and Miss L.J.Charles*
1975	M.C.Riessen and Mrs.B.M.Court *A.J.Stone and Miss B.F.Stove*
1976	A.D.Roche and Miss F.G.Durr *R.L.Stockton and Miss R.Casals*
1977	R.A.J.Hewitt and Miss G.R.Stevens *F.D.McMillan and Miss B.F.Stove*
1978	F.D.McMillan and Miss B.F.Stove *R.O.Ruffels and Mrs.L.W.King*
1979	R.A.J.Hewitt and Miss G.R.Stevens *F.D.McMillan and Miss B.F.Stove*
1980	J.R.Austin and Miss T.A.Austin *M.R.Edmondson and Miss D.L.Fromholtz*
1981	F.D.McMillan and Miss B.F.Stove *J.R.Austin and Miss T.A.Austin*
1982	K.M.Curren and Miss A.E.Smith *J.M.Lloyd and Miss W.M.Turnbull*
1983	J.M.Lloyd and Miss W.M.Turnbull *S.B.Denton and Mrs.L.W.King*
1984	J.M.Lloyd and Miss W.M.Turnbull *S.B.Denton and Miss K.Jordan*
1985	P.F.McNamee and Miss M.Navratilova *J.B.Fitzgerald and Mrs.P.D.Smylie*
1986	K.E.Flach and Miss K.Jordan *H.P.Guenthardt and Miss M.Navratilova*
1987	M.J.Bates and Miss J.M.Durie *D.A.Cahill and Miss N.A-L.Provis*
1988	S.E.Stewart and Miss Z.L.Garrison *K.L.Jones and Mrs.S.W.Magers*
1989	J.R.Pugh and Miss J.Novotna *M.Kratzmann and Miss J.M.Byrne*
1990	R.D.Leach and Miss Z.L.Garrison *J.B.Fitzgerald and Mrs.P.D.Smylie*
1991	J.B.Fitzgerald and Mrs.P.D.Smylie *J.R.Pugh and Miss N.M.Zvereva*
1992	C.Suk and Mrs.A.Neiland *J.F.Eltingh and Miss M.J.M.M.Oremans*
1993	M.R.Woodforde and Miss M.Navratilova *T.J.C.M.Nijssen and Miss M.M.Bollegraf*
1994	T.A.Woodbridge and Miss H.Sukova *T.J.Middleton and Miss L.M.McNeil*
1995	J.A.Stark and Miss M.Navratilova *C.Suk and Miss B.C.Fernandez*
1996	C.Suk and Miss H.Sukova *M.R.Woodforde and Mrs.A.Neiland*
1997	C.Suk and Miss H.Sukova *A.Olhovskiy and Mrs.A.Neiland*
1998	M.N.Mirnyi and Miss S.J.Williams *M.S.Bhupathi and Miss M.Lucic*
1999	L.A.Paes and Miss L.M.Raymond *J.L.Bjorkman and Miss A.S.Kournikova*
2000	D.J.Johnson and Miss K.Y.Po *L.G.Hewitt and Miss K.Clijsters*
2001	L.Friedl and Miss D.Hantuchova *M.C.Bryan and Mrs.A.Huber*
2002	M.S.Bhupathi and Miss E.Likhovtseva *K.R.Ullyett and Miss D.Hantuchova*
2003	L.A.Paes and Miss M.Navratilova *A.Ram and Miss A.Rodionova*
2004	W.Black and Miss C.C.Black *T.A.Woodbridge and Miss A.H.Molik*
2005	M.S.Bhupathi and Miss M.C.Pierce *P.Hanley and Miss T.Perebiynis*
2006	A.Ram and Miss V.Zvonareva *R.C.Bryan and Miss V.E.S.Williams*
2007	J.R.Murray and Miss J.Jankovic *J.L.Bjorkman and Miss A.H.Molik*
2008	R.C.Bryan and Miss S.J.Stosur *M.C.Bryan and Miss K.Srebotnik*
2009	M.S.Knowles and Miss A-L.Groenefeld *L.A.Paes and Miss C.C.Black*
2010	L.A.Paes and Miss C.C.Black *W.A.Moodie and Miss L.M.Raymond*
2011	J.Melzer and Miss I.Benesova *M.S.Bhupathi and Miss E.S.Vesnina*
2012	M.Bryan and Miss L.M.Raymond *L.A.Paes and Miss E.S.Vesnina*
2013	D.M.Nestor and Miss K.Mladenovic *B.Soares and Miss L.M.Raymond*
2014	N.Zimonjic and Miss S.Stosur *M.N.Mirnyi and Miss H.Chan*

BOYS' SINGLES

1947 K.Nielsen *S.V.Davidson*	1964 I.El Shafei *V.Korotkov*	1981 M.W.Anger *P.H.Cash*	1998 R.Federer *I.Labadze*
1948 S.O.Stockenberg *D.Vad*	1965 V.Korotkov *G.Goven*	1982 P.H.Cash *H.Sundstrom*	1999 J.Melzer *K.Pless*
1949 S.O.Stockenberg *J.A.T.Horn*	1966 V.Korotkov *B.E.Fairlie*	1983 S.B.Edberg *J.Frawley*	2000 N.P.A.Mahut *M.Ancic*
1950 J.A.T.Horn *K.Mobarek*	1967 M.Orantes *M.S.Estep*	1984 M.Kratzmann *S.Kruger*	2001 R.Valent *G.Muller*
1951 J.Kupferburger *K.Mobarek*	1968 J.G.Alexander *J.Thamin*	1985 L.Lavalle *E.Velez*	2002 T.C.Reid *L.Quahab*
1952 R.K.Wilson *T.T.Fancutt*	1969 B.M.Bertram *J.G.Alexander*	1986 E.Velez *J.Sanchez*	2003 F.Mergea *C.Guccione*
1953 W.A.Knight *R.Krishnan*	1970 B.M.Bertram *F.Gebert*	1987 D.Nargiso *J.R.Stoltenberg*	2004 G.Monfils *M.Kasiri*
1954 R.Krishnan *A.J.Cooper*	1971 R.I.Kreiss *S.A.Warboys*	1988 N.Pereira *G.Raoux*	2005 J.Chardy *R.Haase*
1955 M.P.Hann *J.E.Lundquist*	1972 B.R.Borg *C.J.Mottram*	1989 L.J.N.Kulti *T.A.Woodbridge*	2006 T.De Bakker *M.Gawron*
1956 R.E.Holmberg *R.G.Laver*	1973 W.W.Martin *C.S.Dowdeswell*	1990 L.A.Paes *M.Ondruska*	2007 D.Young *V.Ignatic*
1957 J.I.Tattersall *I.Ribeiro*	1974 W.W.Martin *Ash Amritraj*	1991 K.J.T.Enquist *M.Joyce*	2008 G.Dimitrov *H.Kontinen*
1958 E.H.Buchholz *P.J.Lall*	1975 C.J.Lewis *R.Ycaza*	1992 D.Skoch *B.Dunn*	2009 A.Kuznetsov *J.Cox*
1959 T.Lejus *R.W.Barnes*	1976 H.P.Guenthardt *P.Elter*	1993 R.Sabau *J.Szymanski*	2010 M.Fucsovics *B.Mitchell*
1960 A.R.Mandelstam *J.Mukerjea*	1977 V.A.W.Winitsky *T.E.Teltscher*	1994 S.M.Humphries *M.A.Philippoussis*	2011 L.Saville *L.Broady*
1961 C.E.Graebner *E.Blanke*	1978 I.Lendl *J.Turpin*	1995 O.Mutis *N.Kiefer*	2012 F.Peliwo *L.Saville*
1962 S.J.Matthews *A.Metreveli*	1979 R.Krishnan *D.Siegler*	1996 V.Voltchkov *I.Ljubicic*	2013 G.Quinzi *H.Chung*
1963 N.Kalogeropoulos *I.El Shafei*	1980 T.Tulasne *H.D.Beutel*	1997 W.Whitehouse *D.Elsner*	2014 N.Rubin *S.Kozlov*

BOYS' DOUBLES

1982 P.H.Cash and J.Frawley *R.D.Leach and J.J.Ross*	1996 D.Bracciali and J.Robichaud *D.Roberts and W.Whitehouse*	2010 L.Broady and T.Farquharson *L.Burton and G.Morgan*
1983 M.Kratzmann and S.Youl *M.Nastase and O. Rahnasto*	1997 L.Horna and N.Massu *J.Van de Westhuizen and W.Whitehouse*	2011 G.Morgan and M.Pavic *O.Golding and J.Vesely*
1984 R.Brown and R.V.Weiss *M.Kratzmann and J.Svensson*	1998 R.Federer and O.L.P.Rochus *M.Llodra and A.Ram*	2012 A.Harris and N.Kyrgios *M.Donati and P.Licciardi*
1985 A.Moreno and J.Yzaga *P.Korda and C.Suk*	1999 G.Coria and D.P.Nalbandian *T.Enev and J.Nieminem*	2013 T.Kokkinakis and N.Kyrgios *E.Couacaud and S.Napolitano*
1986 T.Carbonell and P.Korda *S.Barr and H.Karrasch*	2000 D.Coene and K.Vliegen *A.Banks and B.Riby*	2014 O.Luz and M.Zormann *S.Kozlov and A.Rublev*
1987 J.Stoltenberg and T.A.Woodbridge *D.Nargiso and E.Rossi*	2001 F.Dancevic and G.Lapentti *B.Echagaray and S.Gonzales*	
1988 J.R.Stoltenberg and T.A.Woodbridge *D.Rikl and T.Zdrazila*	2002 F.Mergea and H.V.Tecau *B.Baker and B.Ram*	
1989 J.E.Palmer and J.A.Stark *J-L.De Jager and W.R.Ferreira*	2003 F.Mergea and H.V.Tecau *A.Feeney and C.Guccione*	
1990 S.Lareau and S.Leblanc *C.Marsh and M.Ondruska*	2004 B.Evans and S.Oudsema *R.Haase and V.Troicki*	
1991 K.Alami and G.Rusedski *J-L.De Jager and A.Medvedev*	2005 J.Levine and M.Shabaz *S.Groth and A.Kennaugh*	
1992 S.Baldas and S.Draper *M.S.Bhupathi and N.Kirtane*	2006 K.Damico and N.Schnugg *M.Klizan and A.Martin*	
1993 S.Downs and J.Greenhalgh *N.Godwin and G.Williams*	2007 D.Lopez and M.Trevisan *R.Jebavy and M.Klizan*	
1994 B.Ellwood and M.Philippoussis *V.Platenik and R.Schlachter*	2008 C-P.Hsieh and T-H.Yang *M.Reid and B.Tomic*	
1995 J.Lee and J.M.Trotman *A.Hernandez and M.Puerta*	2009 P-H.Herbert and K.Krawietz *J.Obry and A.Puget*	

GIRLS' SINGLES

1947 Miss G.Domken
Miss B.Wallen
1948 Miss O.Miskova
Miss V.Rigollet
1949 Miss C.Mercelis
Miss J.S.V.Partridge
1950 Miss L.Cornell
Miss A. Winter
1951 Miss L.Cornell
Miss S.Lazzarino
1952 Miss F.J.I.ten Bosch
Miss R.Davar
1953 Miss D.Kilian
Miss V.A.Pitt
1954 Miss V.A.Pitt
Miss C.Monnot
1955 Miss S.M.Armstrong
Miss B.de Chambure
1956 Miss A.S.Haydon
Miss I.Buding
1957 Miss M.G.Arnold
Miss E.Reyes
1958 Miss S.M.Moore
Miss A.Dmitrieva
1959 Miss J.Cross
Miss D.Schuster
1960 Miss K.J.Hantze
Miss L.M Hutchings
1961 Miss G.Baksheeva
Miss K.D.Chabot
1962 Miss G.Baksheeva
Miss E.P.Terry
1963 Miss D.M.Salfati
Miss K.Dening

1964 Miss J.M.Bartkowicz
Miss E.Subirats
1965 Miss O.V.Morozova
Miss R.Giscarfe
1966 Miss B.Lindstrom
Miss J.A.Congdon
1967 Miss J.H.Salome
Miss E.M.Strandberg
1968 Miss K.S.Pigeon
Miss L.E.Hunt
1969 Miss K.Sawamatsu
Miss B.I.Kirk
1970 Miss S.A.Walsh
Miss M.V.Kroshina
1971 Miss M.V.Kroschina
Miss S.H.Minford
1972 Miss I.S.Kloss
Miss G.L.Coles
1973 Miss A.K.Kiyomura
Miss M.Navratilova
1974 Miss M.Jausovec
Miss M.Simionescu
1975 Miss N.Y.Chmyreva
Miss R.Marsikova
1976 Miss N.Y.Chmyreva
Miss M.Kruger
1977 Miss L.Antonoplis
Miss M. Louie
1978 Miss T.A.Austin
Miss H.Mandlikova
1979 Miss M.L.Piatek
Miss A.A.Moulton
1980 Miss D.Freeman
Miss S.J.Leo

1981 Miss Z.L.Garrison
Miss R.R.Uys
1982 Miss C.Tanvier
Miss H.Sukova
1983 Miss P.Paradis
Miss P.Hy
1984 Miss A.N.Croft
Miss E.Reinach
1985 Miss A.Holikova
Miss J.M.Byrne
1986 Miss N.M.Zvereva
Miss L.Meskhi
1987 Miss N.M.Zvereva
Miss J.Halard
1988 Miss B.A.M.Schultz
Miss E.Derly
1989 Miss A.Strnadova
Miss M.J.McGrath
1990 Miss A.Strnadova
Miss K.Sharpe
1991 Miss B.Rittner
Miss E.Makarova
1992 Miss C.R.Rubin
Miss L.Courtois
1993 Miss N.Feber
Miss R.Grande
1994 Miss M.Hingis
Miss M-R.Jeon
1995 Miss A.Olsza
Miss T.Tanasugarn
1996 Miss A.Mauresmo
Miss M.L.Serna
1997 Miss C.C.Black
Miss A.Rippner

1998 Miss K.Srebotnik
Miss K.Clijsters
1999 Miss I.Tulyagnova
Miss L.Krasnoroutskaya
2000 Miss M.E.Salerni
Miss T.Perebiynis
2001 Miss A.Widjaja
Miss D.Safina
2002 Miss V.Douchevina
Miss M.Sharapova
2003 Miss K.Flipkens
Miss A.Tchakvetadze
2004 Miss K.Bondarenko
Miss A.Ivanovic
2005 Miss A.R.Radwanska
Miss T.Paszek
2006 Miss C.Wozniacki
Miss M.Rybarikova
2007 Miss U.Radwanska
Miss M.Brengle
2008 Miss L.M.D.Robson
Miss N.Lertcheewakarn
2009 Miss N.Lertcheewakarn
Miss K.Mladenovic
2010 Miss K.Pliskova
Miss S.Ishizu
2011 Miss A.Barty
Miss I.Khromacheva
2012 Miss E.Bouchard
Miss E.Svitolina
2013 Miss B.Bencic
Miss T.Townsend
2014 Miss J.Ostapenko
Miss K.Schmiedlova

GIRLS' DOUBLES

1982 Miss E.A.Herr and Miss P.Barg
Miss B.S.Gerken and Miss G.A.Rush
1983 Miss P.A.Fendick and Miss P.Hy
Miss C.Anderholm and Miss H.Olsson
1984 Miss C.Kuhlman and Miss S.C.Rehe
Miss V.Milvidskaya and Miss L.I.Savchenko
1985 Miss L.Field and Miss J.G.Thompson
Miss E.Reinach and Miss J.A.Richardson
1986 Miss M.Jaggard and Miss L.O'Neill
Miss L.Meskhi and Miss N.M.Zvereva
1987 Miss N.Medvedeva and Miss N.M.Zvereva
Miss I.S.Kim and Miss P.M.Moreno
1988 Miss J.A.Faull and Miss R.McQuillan
Miss A.Dechaume and Miss E.Derly
1989 Miss J.M.Capriati and Miss M.J.McGrath
Miss A.Strnadova and Miss E.Sviglerova
1990 Miss K.Habsudova and Miss A.Strnadova
Miss N.J.Pratt and Miss K.Sharpe
1991 Miss C.Barclay and Miss L.Zaltz
Miss J.Limmer and Miss A.Woolcock
1992 Miss M.Avotins and Miss L.McShea
Miss P.Nelson and Miss J.Steven
1993 Miss L.Courtois and Miss N.Feber
Miss H.Mochizuki and Miss Y.Yoshida

1994 Miss E.De Villiers and Miss E.E.Jelfs
Miss C.M.Morariu and Miss L.Varmuzova
1995 Miss C.C.Black and Miss A.Olsza
Miss T.Musgrove and Miss J. Richardson
1996 Miss O.Barabanschikova and Miss A.Mauresmo
Miss L.Osterloh and Miss S.Reeves
1997 Miss C.C.Black and Miss I.Selyutina
Miss M.Matevzic and Miss K.Srebotnik
1998 Miss E.Dyrberg and Miss J.Kostanic
Miss P.Rampre and Miss I.Tulyaganova
1999 Miss D.Bedanova and Miss M.E.Salerni
Miss T.Perebiynis and Miss I.Tulyaganova
2000 Miss I.Gaspar and Miss T.Perebiynis
Miss D.Bedanova and Miss M.E.Salerni
2001 Miss G.Dulko and Miss A.Harkleroad
Miss C.Horiatopoulos and Miss B.Mattek
2002 Miss E.Clijsters and Miss B.Strycova
Miss A.Baker and Miss A-L.Groenfeld
2003 Miss A.Kleybanova and Miss S.Mirza
Miss K.Bohmova and Miss M.Krajicek
2004 Miss V.A.Azarenka and Miss V.Havartsova
Miss M.Erakovic and Miss M.Niculescu

2005 Miss V.A.Azarenka and Miss A.Szavay
Miss M.Erakovic and Miss M.Niculescu
2006 Miss A.Kleybanova and Miss A.Pavlyuchenkova
Miss K.Antoniychuk and Miss A.Dulgheru
2007 Miss A.Pavlyuchenkova and Miss U.Radwanska
Miss M.Doi and Miss K.Nara
2008 Miss P.Hercog and Miss J.Moore
Miss I.Holland and Miss S.Peers
2009 Miss N.Lertcheewakarn and Miss S.Peers
Miss K.Mladenovic and Miss S.Njiric
2010 Miss T.Babos and Miss S.Stephens
Miss I.Khromacheva and Miss E.Svitolina
2011 Miss E.Bouchard and Miss G.Min
Miss D.Schuurs and Miss H.C. Tang
2012 Miss E.Bouchard and Miss T.Townsend
Miss B.Bencic and Miss A.Konjuh
2013 Miss B.Krejcikova and Miss K.Siniakova
Miss A.Kalinina and Miss I.Shymanovich
2014 Miss T.Grende and Miss Q.Ye
Miss M.Bouzkova and Miss D.Galfi

ROLEX

The Rolex Wimbledon Picture of the Year Competition 2014

Winner

Gael Monfils at full stretch in the air as he tries to make a
volley during The Championships 2014

Photographer

Mike Frey
Tennishead Magazine